D1217631

Milton and Homer:
"Written to Aftertimes"

Medieval & Renaissance Literary Studies

General Editor:
Richard J. DuRocher

Editorial Board:
Judith H. Anderson
Diana Treviño Benet
Donald Cheney
Ann Baynes Coiro
Mary T. Crane
Patrick Cullen
A. C. Hamilton
Margaret P. Hannay
Michael Lieb
Thomas P. Roche Jr.
Mary Beth Rose
John M. Steadman
Humphrey Tonkin
Susanne Woods

Originally titled the *Duquesne Studies: Philological Series* (and later renamed the *Language & Literature Series*), the **Medieval & Renaissance Literary Studies Series** has been published by Duquesne University Press since 1960. This publishing endeavor seeks to promote the study of late medieval, Renaissance, and seventeenth century English literature by presenting scholarly and critical monographs, collections of essays, editions, and compilations. The series encourages a broad range of interpretation, including the relationship of literature and its cultural contexts, close textual analysis, and the use of contemporary critical methodologies.

Foster Provost
EDITOR, 1960–1984

Albert C. Labriola
EDITOR, 1985–2009

Richard J. DuRocher
EDITOR, 2010

MILTON AND HOMER

"WRITTEN TO AFTERTIMES"

Gregory Machacek

DUQUESNE UNIVERSITY PRESS
Pittsburgh, Pennsylvania

PR3562
.M23
2011
cop. 3

o 754770718

Copyright © 2011 Duquesne University Press
All rights reserved

Published in the United States of America by
DUQUESNE UNIVERSITY PRESS
600 Forbes Avenue
Pittsburgh, Pennsylvania 15282

No part of this book may be used or reproduced,
in any manner or form whatsoever,
without written permission from the publisher,
except in the case of short quotations
in critical articles or reviews.

Chapter 3 originally appeared in *Cithara: Studies in the Judeo-Christian Tradition*, 40:1 (Nov. 2000): 37–48; I am grateful for permission to reprint. A portion of chapter 1 originally appeared in *PMLA*, 122:2 (March 2007): 522–36. A version of chapter 4 originally appeared in *Figures of Bloom: The Salt Companion to Harold Bloom*, ed. Roy Sellars and Graham Allen (Cambridge: Salt, 2007), 183–98.

Library of Congress Cataloging-in-Publication Data

Machacek, Gregory.
    Milton and Homer: "written to aftertimes" / Gregory Machacek.
        p. cm. — (Medieval & Renaissance literary studies)
    Summary: "Explores the various ways in which Homer's epic poems influenced Milton in his own ambition to compose an enduring, canonical work of literature. Machacek's study of this major interpoetic relationship is methodologically responsive to the historicist critical enterprise dominant within literary study for the past three decades" — Provided by publisher.
    Includes bibliographical references and index.
    ISBN 978-0-8207-0447-0 (acid-free paper)
    1. Milton, John, 1608–1674. Paradise lost. 2. Milton, John, 1608–1674 — Sources. 3. Homer — Influence. 4. English poetry — Greek influences. 5. Intertextuality. I. Title.

    PR3562.M23 2011
    821'.4 — dc23

                                                        2011028585

∞ Printed on acid-free paper.

For Maya

οὐ μὲν γὰρ τοῦ γε κρεῖσσον καὶ ἄρειον
ἢ ὅθ᾽ ὁμοφρονέοντε νοήμασιν οἶκον ἔχητον
ἀνὴρ ἠδὲ γυνή. (*Odyssey* 6. 182–84)

CONTENTS

Acknowledgments

I thank Mary Ann Radzinowicz and Piero Pucci for early guidance on this project. I am thankful to Al Labriola, John Mulryan, Susanne Woods, Christine Perkell, John King, and John Leonard for providing forums in which I could develop the ideas in the book.

I must express my profound gratitude for the efforts that Richard DuRocher made, even in the final months of his battle with cancer, to help me improve my manuscript.

This book began as a dissertation under the direction of Gordon Teskey. At every stage of its development, I have benefited from his precept and example, his insight, advice, and direction, and I have been bolstered by the persistence of his belief in this undertaking.

I thank Marist College for sabbatical support that allowed me to make significant progress in my research.

I thank my editors at Duquesne University Press, particularly Kathy Meyer, for their attention and care with my manuscript.

My deepest debt of gratitude is to my wife, Maya. I would like to thank her for her unwavering support and unwearying encouragement. We may no longer believe that "nothing lovelier can be found / In Woman, than...Good works in her husband to promote," but where that loveliness *is* found, among however many others, it surely still warrants appreciation.

Introduction

This book examines how the Homeric epics figured in the composition of *Paradise Lost*. Miltonists in the late twentieth century tended to see the influence of Homer on Milton's epic as minimal, at least by comparison with that of Virgil. Davis P. Harding established the contemporary orthodoxy, claiming, "it must be clear to every reader that by far the most significant classical influence on *Paradise Lost* is the *Aeneid* of Virgil." Charles Martindale similarly asserts, "recognizing the passing Homeric echoes—for those who do—is hardly among the more intense pleasures of reading *Paradise Lost*. Such echoes are in fact comparatively infrequent." And William Porter claims, "Milton almost always sees Homer *through* Vergil."[1]

Milton's earliest critics, by contrast, regarded Homer as the key precursor. John Ward's letter of 1738, reporting an interview with Milton's daughter Deborah, mentions that Homer was one of Milton's three favorite authors (along with Isaiah and Ovid).[2] Toland's biography says of Milton, "he has incontestably exceeded the fecundity of Homer, whose Two Poems he could almost repeat without book."[3] Jonathan Richardson Sr. describes Milton as having "a most Intimate Knowledge of All the Poets worthy his Notice, Ancient or Modern; Chiefly the Best, and above All Homer."[4] One of Milton's daughters, Samuel Johnson reports, "represented him as most delighting [in] Homer, which he could almost repeat."[5] Joseph Addison, who considers *Paradise*

Lost in connection with earlier epics, often focuses on ways in which Milton resembles Homer specifically: "no Poet seems ever to have studied Homer more, or to have more resembled him in the greatness of Genius than Milton."[6] In *Spectator* paper 285, he asserts, "Milton has copied after Homer, rather than Virgil, in the length of his periods, the copiousness of his phrases, and the running of his verses into one another."[7] Johnson similarly twice pairs Milton and Homer in a way that excludes Virgil altogether, claiming that Milton's "work is not the greatest of heroic poems, only because it is not the first," and that "considered with respect to design [*Paradise Lost*] may claim first place, and with respect to performance, the second [to the *Iliad*], among the productions of the human mind."[8] John Henry Todd's *Variorum* meticulously catalogs the many passages in Milton that echo phrases or lines in the *Iliad* and the *Odyssey*.[9]

I believe that twentieth century Miltonists formed an estimate of the importance of Homer to Milton so different from that of earlier critics largely because the study of allusion in the twentieth century was almost exclusively hermeneutic in its focus, whereas earlier critics, as some of the quotations in the previous paragraph indicate, were as much interested in issues of composition and literary status as they were in issues of meaning. In the ensuing chapters, I consider many of Milton's allusions to the *Iliad* and the *Odyssey*. But the usual focus of allusion studies — how particular allusions reinforce or qualify the meaning of specific passages — is only a small part of my concern here. My thesis is that the Homeric epics provided Milton with more than just a resource for enriching the significance of various passages in *Paradise Lost*; they provided him with guidance in his efforts to write an enduring work of literature, to "leave something so written to aftertimes, as they should not willingly let it die."[10] I argue that Milton's attempt to write what we today call a canonical work of literature was influenced by the way in which the Homeric epics were being canonically reproduced within early modern European culture.

In order to make that argument, I must expand the scope of allusion study as it has traditionally been practiced. As I have mentioned, the study of allusion has of late been largely, and in many cases exclusively, hermeneutic in orientation. This hermeneutic focus of traditional allusion studies is well illustrated in an examination of Milton's relation to the classical tradition of epic, William Porter's *Reading the Classics and Paradise Lost,* and in G. W. Pigman's learned survey of "Varieties of Imitation in the Renaissance." In preparation for his study of Milton, Porter sets out a taxonomy of "literary associations." Certain of these associations—the ones he calls appropriations, reminiscences, echoes, and borrowings—are for him "lesser forms of literary intertextuality" precisely because they do not enrich the *meaning* of Milton's epic. His book focuses on what he terms "critical allusions," which are defined as those that possess "extraordinary hermeneutic importance." Forms of association that do not aid in the interpretation of Milton's poem are for Porter "inherently uninteresting."[11] Pigman similarly approaches Renaissance theories of imitation with the assumption that they will provide "guidance for the interpretation of Renaissance literature."[12]

Pigman seems frustrated that he is able to generate only a "less than inspiring [hermeneutic] principle"; that "a reader must be very cautious in even calling a similarity between two texts an imitation or an allusion, much less in analyzing the use or significance of the similarity."[13] And for his part, although the index to the Columbia edition of Milton's works catalogs 183 allusions to Homer in Milton's epic, Porter asserts there is only "one critical allusion to Homer in *Paradise Lost.*" (The one he isolates is Satan's "Better to reign in hell than serve in Heav'n," which recalls, and reverses, the comment that the shade of Achilles makes to Odysseus when the two meet in the underworld: "I'd rather follow the plow as thrall to another...than be a king over all the perished dead").[14] Otherwise, Porter finds himself "left with the feeling that Homer's texts in Milton's allusions are called upon more for their prestige than their proper content."[15]

But, largely as a result of the debate over the canon, issues of prestige have again come to possess tremendous interest for literary scholars. That renewed critical interest in issues of literary status, prestige, and reputation provides the context for the following examination of how the Homeric epics guided Milton's efforts to compose a poem that successive generations would continue to value. This study ranges, then, from the most minute form of intertextual relation, the verbal echo, to the broadest: the status relative to one another of particular texts within the literary canon. By broadening our understanding of the effects that allusions can have and the poetic uses to which they can be put, we can gain a richer understanding of this dimension of Homer's importance to Milton. While I will argue against Porter that more than just one of Milton's allusions to Homer serves to enrich the meaning of his epic, I will also explore how those allusions serve purposes other than simply reinforcing or qualifying the significance of particular passages in the epic, particularly how they were involved in establishing Milton's canonical status.

However frustrating Pigman finds it to derive principles of *interpretation* from Renaissance theories of imitation, the excerpts he collects testify that Renaissance theorists thought about imitation primarily in terms of literary *status*, of the relative merit of earlier and later texts. One of the three main categories into which he sorts metaphors of imitation is *aemulatio*, eristic rivalry; and even in the case of less antagonistic forms of imitation, he documents the theorists' recurrent concern with qualitative issues: with how well or poorly the imitation is managed. For a Renaissance author, imitation was a matter not so much of the meaning of the work, as of its merit: "behind/in front of, worse/better."[16]

That such evaluative concerns are appropriate, even crucial, to a consideration of Milton's relation to Homer is evident from the fact that (as Porter notes), "Homer himself is mentioned once in *Paradise Lost*, an honor Virgil does not share"—and from the fact that that mention includes a reference precisely to Homer's enduring prestige.[17] In the passage that Porter has in mind, in the proem to book 3, Milton mentions that he often recalls "blind Maeonides" as being "equal'd with me in [the] fate" of blindness, then adds his wish that he might also be "equal'd with [him] in *renown*" (33–35; emphasis added). As Stephen Fallon puts it, Milton here "aspires to the fame of Thamyris and Homer."[18] In these lines, Milton characterizes Homer's epics less as subtexts that can meaningfully resonate with his own poem than as examples of poems that have been revered for a very long time and that might therefore teach him something about how to create an enduring poem.

In order to expand the scope of allusion study beyond its traditional hermeneutic focus so that it can speak to issues of literary prestige, renown, and canonicity, I will put it in communication with certain strains of poststructuralist literary theory, particularly the historically and culturally oriented studies predominant within literary criticism since the 1980s and the insights by scholars such as Barbara Herrnstein Smith and John Guillory into the process of canon formation. Theoretical treatments of allusion have generally emerged out of a formalist perspective, and even in relatively recent treatments of the phenomenon, such as Joseph Pucci's *The Full-Knowing Reader*, one detects a hostility, or at least disinclination, toward historically or culturally oriented literary criticism: "But I hear now (and listen) to other voices championing a cultural turn in literary studies, telling me that the 'sonnets on the beauty of the forest make a new kind of sense next to the language of timber legislation and advertisements by timber and environmental lobbies are best understood in terms of their reliance on complex narratives of progress and conservation.' . . . Yet . . . I don't happen to believe that it is the best sense to be gotten where literature is concerned."[19]

The disrespect is mutual; poststructuralist theorists have often presented their concepts by contrasting them with traditional approaches to allusion. Jonathan Culler, citing the Kristevan provenance of the term *intertextuality* has argued that "source study of a traditional and positivistic kind" is precisely what the newer concept was "designed to transcend."[20] Kristeva herself regards the common use of *intertextuality* as a synonym for *allusiveness* as a misappropriation of her term.[21] Harold Bloom asserts that verbal echoes have "almost nothing to do with...poetic influence, in the sense [he] gives to it" and are suited only to "those carrion-eaters of scholarship, the source hunters."[22] Even when poststructuralist critics do not adopt such a dismissive stance toward allusion, they sometimes characterize their own projects by contrasting them with approaches that involve the study of allusion. Louis Montrose, for example, describes new historicism as a project that "reorients the axis of intertextuality, substituting for the diachronic text of an autonomous literary history the synchronic text of a cultural system."[23]

But this antagonism between allusion studies and poststructuralist criticism is unnecessary. Intertextuality and allusion are actually complementary concepts that, taken together, provide a more comprehensive view of literary relations than either of them alone. It is true that there are irreducible differences between allusion as traditionally understood and such poststructuralist concepts as intertextuality, influence, and cultural materialism. But once the phenomenon of allusion has been carefully distinguished from a concept like intertextuality, the two may then be coordinated to foster a richer understanding of textual interrelations than either concept alone allows, an understanding that can sharpen our insights into texts and cultural contexts by allowing fluid movement between Montrose's diachronic axis of literary history and synchronic axis of cultural systems, rather than treating the two as contrasting and mutually exclusive alternatives.

My opening chapter sketches how such a coordination of allusion and intertextuality might be effected, and the book as a whole may be understood as fleshing out that sketch. In each subsequent chapter, I combine the diachronic analysis of traditional allusion study with the synchronic analysis of cultural studies by considering Milton's allusions to Homer in the context of various presuppositions of early modern culture, especially those presuppositions that bear on the status (what contemporary scholars call the "canonicity") of literary texts.

In addition to distinguishing allusion from intertextuality, the opening chapter also treats allusion in its own right, attempting to clarify aspects of the phenomenon that previous treatments have left confused. The study of allusion, even apart from its having been dismissed by poststructuralist theorists as positivist and obsolete, has been hampered by conceptual murkiness and terminological imprecision, as well as by the limiting assumption I mentioned above: that allusion study should be exclusively hermeneutic in its focus. In order to facilitate the analyses in the subsequent chapters, I offer in the first chapter a number of conceptual and terminological clarifications regarding the phraseological appropriations that we generally call allusions or echoes; moreover, I reflect briefly on the range of effects that such phraseological adaptations may have, or purposes to which they may be put, besides enriching the significance of the passages in which they occur. This effort more fully to understand the phenomenon of allusion in its own right continues throughout the book; the allusive relationship between Milton and Homer provides the occasion for an extended reflection on the nature of allusion generally speaking.

The book thus has two complementary aims: on the one hand, employing an enriched understanding of the phenomenon of allusion, I offer an account of the relation between Milton and Homer; on the other hand, I use my examination of the relation between Milton and Homer as an opportunity to refine further our understanding of the nature of allusion. Most chapters do both: they extend the general theorization of allusion begun in chapter 1, and they advance my argument regarding the nature of the relationship between Milton and Homer specifically; namely, that the way in which Homer's works were being reproduced within the early modern period provided Milton guidance in how he might himself create an enduring work of literature.

The account of the relation between Milton and Homer focuses on what I will call the institutional and discursive mechanisms of canonization operative in the mid- to late seventeenth century. Every age has a set of ideas and terms by which literary texts are assigned cultural value. A new text will acquire and maintain status based in part on how it conforms to cultural assumptions or presuppositions partly discernible in this evaluative nomenclature. (I occasionally use the admittedly cumbersome phrase "discursive mechanism of canonization" for these terms of literary approbation to put an emphasis not just on the terms themselves but on how they functioned within early modern aesthetic ideology.) Like Stephen Dobranski, who argues that Milton authored his works with a sophisticated and nuanced understanding of the nature of the book trade of his day, I will show that Milton was also extremely savvy regarding the principles by which literary works elicited efforts of preservation and dissemination and thereby secured enduring value, what we today call *canonicity*.[24]

In Milton's age, for example, it was expected that a great work of literature would be exemplary, in the sense of setting forth pointed moral exempla. Accordingly, Milton's literary ambitions, as he revealed them in *The Reason of Church Government*, were to compose a work that might be "doctrinal and *exemplary* to a Nation...teaching over the whole book of sanctity and vertu through all the instances of *example*" (CM 3:237–39; emphasis added). In chapter 2, I undertake a close examination of the Homeric allusions in book 6 of *Paradise Lost* in an effort to reclassify the war in heaven episode—as one of the moral exempla of which Renaissance literary theory held heroic poems should be composed. Modern critics have had difficulty classifying the episode because it contains both epic and mock-epic strains. I argue that their difficulty in classifying the episode results from them categorizing it generically, when it should be classified rhetorically. The war in heaven is best regarded as an exemplum—or, more precisely, as an extended minatory exemplum with a contrasting hortatory example (that of Abdiel) incorporated into it. A negative exemplum presents a figure whose behavior is to be avoided, and it must thus negotiate contradictory demands. It must present that figure's actions as serious and yet condemn them. It must respect without seeming to honor. And this, I think, explains the mix of epic and mock-epic strains that have made the episode so difficult to categorize generically: Satan must be made to appear an epic threat, yet be dismissed with mocking scorn.

Accordingly, Milton's allusions to Homer in books 5 and 6 of *Paradise Lost* run a range from respectfully imitative to pointedly critical. Verbal echoes, as Milton's practice in this episode allows us to see, always have an evaluative dimension, implicitly lauding or condemning the values celebrated in the text to which they allude. And in the war in heaven episode, Milton exploits that dimension of allusion to engage his reader in a sustained critical evaluation of the ethic enshrined in the Homeric epics.

Chapter 3 considers the status of *Paradise Lost* as a Christian epic. As Thomas Greene, John Steadman, and Judith Kates show, the notion of a "Christian epic" was formulated by Italian theorists in advance of the efforts of Tasso, Vida, and Milton to compose such a work, and thus served as a literary ideal toward which poets of the Renaissance might aspire. In that regard, the term *Christian epic* functions as one of the discursive mechanisms of canonization operative in the early modern period. But as Milton quite clearly saw, "the better fortitude of patience and heroic martyrdom" does not lend itself to narration within a genre that has hitherto deemed "warrs...the only Argument Heroic" (*PL* 9.31–32, 28–29). *Christian epic* is not so much a category enabling artistic production as it is a problem to be solved. I will argue that Milton solved what Judith Kates called the "problem of Christian epic" by radically reconceiving the fundamental characteristics of epic. Rather than following Virgil in seeing a set of martial episodes as defining the genre, Milton finds the essence of the epic genre in a particular aesthetic effect—namely, a mix of the marvelous and the probable—suggested to him by

Tasso's Aristotelian literary theory. But Milton locates this mix in the *style* of his epic, rather than in its *narrative*, as Tasso had done. The density of allusiveness in *Paradise Lost*, which effects in writing some of what Homer's formulaic diction achieves in oral delivery, makes for a style that combines the marvelous and probable, in phraseology that is simultaneously elevated and yet vaguely familiar. Here again, Milton's practice casts into relief an aspect of the workings of allusion generally, revealing that other aspects of an allusion (in this case, the mere sense of familiarity that a reader has when he or she encounters phrases reminiscent of an earlier author's work) can sometimes be as functionally important as its capacity to enrich local meaning.

With their consideration of *exemplum* and *Christian epic*, chapters 2 and 3 are focused on how *Paradise Lost* conforms to canonizing terminology well established by the time Milton began composition of his epic. In chapters 4 and 5, I focus on how *Paradise Lost* takes up its canonical status in connection with terms of literary approbation—*originality* and *sublimity*—just emerging in Milton's day.

In chapter 4, the term on which I focus is *originality*, which has long served as a discursive mechanism operative in the canonization of Milton's works. The term has been particularly important to Harold Bloom, whose "anxiety of influence" represents, like intertextuality, an important poststructuralist concept from which I distinguish, but with which I coordinate, my own understanding of allusion. In this study, Bloom's account of Milton's relation to his precursors provides the pretext for a consideration of historically varying conceptions of origins and originality. The sense of the word *original* as we now generally use the term, the sense of "not imitated from another," was only emerging during Milton's lifetime, and I believe the historically variable meaning of this term helps to explain why Harold Bloom finds it so difficult to account for Milton's poetic practice. I examine the unusual conception of origins implicit within *Paradise Lost* in order both to cast into relief certain aspects of the idea that are characteristic of the post-Enlightenment understanding of originality and to suggest how we might use the transitional, late seventeenth century sense of that concept better to account for the place Milton imagined for his poem within the epic tradition.

One of the primary critical concepts by which the canonization of *Paradise Lost* was effected was a late seventeenth century transformation of the *meraviglia* on which Tasso's theory had focused, namely, the sublime. Conventional literary history dates the emergence of the sublime as a key critical concept from the publication of Nicolas Boileau's translation of Longinus in 1674, the year of Milton's death; but a Greek and Latin edition of Longinus was available in England from 1638, and a translation (by fellow republican John Hall) from 1652. And, of course, in *Of Education* Milton recommends that students read Longinus. Annabel Patterson argues, "Milton himself *intended* his poem to be seen as a demonstration of sublime themes and effects," anticipating this discursive mechanism of his epic's canonization.[25]

Chapter 5 attempts to substantiate Patterson's contention that Milton sought and achieved sublimity *avant la Boileauvian lettre*. I study the way in which Milton's allusions in many cases exponentially surpass their Homeric and Virgilian sources. In addition to the evaluative dimension of allusion that I examine in chapter 3, allusions also establish a rivalry between source and alluding text; indeed, this competitive dimension of interpoetic relations, under the term *aemulatio*, was more important to Renaissance literary theorists than the capacity of allusions to enhance local meaning. But Milton's competitive allusions do more than simply go Homer and Virgil one better; they often achieve a fully Longinian sublimity by suggesting that Milton's cosmos is of an entirely different order of magnitude than those of his epic precursors.

In the final chapter, I shift my focus from discursive to institutional mechanisms of canonization. In *Cultural Capital,* John Guillory argues that in order fully to understand canonicity one must consider the role of institutions in the process by which texts are canonized, and he illustrates that, since the late eighteenth century the institution of the school has been responsible for the preservation and dissemination of literary works. Here again, Milton seems to have anticipated the developments that would be involved in the perpetuation of his epic. Indeed, I argue that he settled on the genre of epic for his great work (after considering drama and ode) in part because he could imagine an institution, the school, in which that work might be preserved and disseminated. *Paradise Lost* shows signs of having been composed with an eye toward its being a school text.

Milton's boast in *Pro populo anglicano defensio* that, despite the poor intrinsic quality of Salmasius's works, they would nevertheless survive because they were in dialogue with his own shows implicitly Milton's recognition that a work's canonical survival is partly a function of its intertextual connections (CM 4.324). This study establishes that his positioning of *Paradise Lost* in connection with the Homeric epics (as they were being appreciated and disseminated in his day) is one of the chief strategies by which Milton ensured that aftertimes would not willingly let his own epic die.

ONE

"By Allusion Called"

Diachronic and Synchronic Intertextuality

At the end of *Paradise Regained,* we are told three times within 20 lines that Satan fell from the tower where he tempted the Son: "Satan smitten with amazement fell" (4.562), "So...the Tempter...Fell" (4.569–71), "So Satan fell" (4.581). Because the word *fell* is repeated three times, and perhaps also because the word *so* begins the second and third iterations, critics have found that this passage recalls the conclusion of the battle between Redcross knight and the dragon in book 1 of *The Faerie Queene,* where, in canto 11, stanza 54, the phrase "So downe he fell" begins lines 1, 3, 5 and 9:

> So downe he fell, and forth his life did breath,
> That vanisht into smoke and cloudes swift;
> So downe he fell, that th'earth him underneath
> Did grone, as feeble so great load to lift;
> So downe he fell, as an huge rocky clift,

Whose false foundacion waves have washt away,
With dreadful poyse is from the mayneland rift,
And rolling downe, great *Neptune* doth dismay;
So downe he fell, and like an heaped mountaine lay.[1]

To note, evaluate, and interpret this sort of brief phraseological imitation of an earlier writer—whether referred to as an *allusion* or an *echo* or an instance of *intertextuality*—has been an aspect of literary scholarship at least since Macrobius cataloged Virgil's borrowings (*furta*) from Homer. However venerable the critical enterprise that studies such imitative phrases may be, discussion of the phenomenon of allusion is beset by limiting assumptions, conceptual murkiness, and terminological imprecision. Worse, the language generally used by critics to describe phraseological adaptations like those of Milton—words like *echo* or *borrowing*—tends to imply unoriginality or slavish imitation, even when the critic means to stress the imitative writer's subtle craft and playful erudition. As a result, scholarly consideration of later authors' imitation, adaptation, and recontextualization of earlier authors' phraseology presently enjoys relatively little prestige within the field of literary study.

The intense theoretical activity that began in the late 1960s—and which has offered new terms like *intertextuality* and radical redefinitions of traditional terms like *influence*—has not done as much as one might expect to introduce conceptual or terminological rigor into our understanding of phraseological imitation. If anything, theorists of intertextuality, opposing their approaches to the traditional study of allusion, have tended to diminish even further the status of such study. In a treatment of the concept of intertextuality, Jonathan Culler suggests that consideration of verbal echoes has essentially been rendered obsolete by the newer concern.[2] Harold Bloom (whose theory of influence I will take up more fully in chapter 4) claims bluntly that verbal echoes have "almost nothing to do with...poetic influence, in the sense [he] gives to it" and are suited only to "those carrion-eaters of scholarship, the source hunters."[3]

Despite such scorn from poststructuralist critics, from at least the early 1980s, scholars of classical and modern literature have been struggling to develop a conceptual model and a critical vocabulary that will allow them more effectively to discuss the nature and workings of these brief phraseological adaptations (usually referred to as *allusions* or *echoes,* though such terms, I will show, must be used with care). Most frequently, critics have proceeded by likening allusion to something else. Richard Garner likens allusions to metaphors, with the allusive text as tenor and the evoked or source text as vehicle. John Hollander likens them to the rhetorical trope of metalepsis. William Porter compares allusion to the logical syllogism known as enthymeme; Allan Pasco, to a horticultural graft. John Hale, citing game theorist Roger Caillois, likens allusive writing to play.[4] Each of these analogies does illuminate some aspect of the phenomenon of verbal echo, but the range and diversity of the phenomena to which allusion has been likened suggests that no single comparison can convey all aspects of this subtle and variform literary device.

I aim to provide a more comprehensive conceptual model of allusion, or phraseological adaptation, than has heretofore been offered (in part by synthesizing the work of the aforementioned critics, who, focused on different authors and periods, often seem unaware of one another's efforts). But rather than propose another illustrative metaphor, I intend to offer a detailed consideration of its nature and workings. To a large extent, this will involve reconsidering the customary critical nomenclature for describing manifestations and aspects of the phenomenon, though I will attempt in that reconsideration to introduce as little technical jargon of my own as possible, in some cases simply defining existing terms more precisely or investing informal vocabulary with a quasi-technical force. In addition to introducing a greater degree of conceptual precision, one goal of my terminological suggestions is to confront the critical predisposition to regard allusion dismissively and its study as a form of pedantry that has been outmoded by newer, more engaging approaches. I hope to put the study of allusion on a better footing within contemporary literary studies. It is true that allusion should be *distinguished* from the poststructuralist concept of intertextuality, but once it has been, and has been understood more completely in its own right, it can (and, in fact, should) be *coordinated* with intertextuality to foster the richest, most comprehensive understanding of the relations between texts.

Intertextuality

For many critics, the term *intertextuality* is essentially synonymous with the term *allusion*. When Jane Melbourne, for example, studies "Biblical Intertextuality in *Samson Agonistes*" or when Anne Lake Prescott examines "Intertextual Topology: English Writers and Pantagruel's Hell," they use the term *intertextuality* to designate what would once have been called *allusions to*, or *echoes*, or *adaptations of* an earlier author's work in the work of some later writer.[5] Their use of the term as a rough synonym for *allusiveness* is fairly characteristic of general critical parlance.

But for some critics, the word has a meaning that is significantly different from, even antithetical to, the more traditional terms. Julia Kristeva coined the term *intertextuality* to designate a special form of textual interrelationship: the way in which texts—and not just works of literature, but other meaningful social phenomena such as carnival—emerge from a particular semiotic order.[6] For her, the word designates not so much the relations between particular literary works as the semiotic principles and presuppositions that lie between texts of all sorts from a given culture and that allow each of them to have meaning for members of that culture. Some critics would like to see the term retain this special meaning. Culler, for example, stresses the difference between, on the one hand, truly intertextual explorations of the "order of words" in which a text takes up its meaning and, on the other hand, "source study of a traditional and positivistic kind." Intertextuality, he insists, is "less a name for a work's

relation to particular *prior* texts than a designation of its participation in the discursive *space* of a culture." Indeed, for Culler, the
concept of intertextuality was expressly "designed to transcend"
that of allusion.[7] Kristeva herself has called the common use of
intertextuality as a rough synonym for *allusiveness* a "banal"
misappropriation of her term.[8]

Nevertheless, in general critical parlance, the term has become
a catchall, referring to various sorts of textual interrelation: the
relations between later authors and their precursors as well as
the relations between texts and the reigning semiotic practices of
a given historical moment. As a result, the original definition of
intertextuality probably cannot at this point be upheld. Indeed, the
"banal" understanding of the term quickly became so widespread
that Kristeva herself coined a new term, *transposition*, to convey
what she had originally designated by the word *intertextuality*.[9]

However, although it may no longer be possible, as Culler
would wish, to insist that the term *intertextuality* retain its original sense, it is nevertheless true that the kind of analysis that
Kristeva and other poststructuralists undertake does differ significantly from the traditional study of allusions and verbal echoes.
The broad distinction is between approaches that study the text
diachronically, in connection with earlier works of literature, and
those that examine the text synchronically, in connection with
a contemporaneous semiotic field made up of both literary and
nonliterary texts. In the essays in which she introduced the term
intertextuality, Kristeva indicates that her project involves plac-
ing "textual arrangements...within the general text (culture) of
which they are a part" and repeatedly stresses that she is as interested in synchronic as anterior utterances.[10] I want ultimately to
argue that the kind of diachronic and hermeneutic investigations
typical of traditional allusion study can (and should) be coordinated with the synchronic, semiotic analyses envisioned in the
early work of Kristeva and other poststructuralists. But that coordination would be premature if it did not first fully acknowledge
how different the newer approaches are from traditional studies

of allusion. I offer below a contained and relatively brief reading of *Paradise Lost* that I believe is in the spirit of the essays in
which Kristeva proposed the concept of intertextuality and that
I hope will illustrate the aims, method, and results of an analysis
that uses the concept of intertextuality in its more limited, original sense.

When one examines Kristeva's expressly intertextual analysis
of a literary text—the reading of Antoine de La Sale's *Jehan de
Saintré* that forms part of her essay "The Bounded Text"—one
sees clearly the way in which her literary insights are subordi-
nated to a synchronically oriented semiotic project: the purpose
of her reading is not to interpret La Sale's story, but to reveal how
it exemplifies what she calls the "ideologeme of the sign," a semiotic order operative in the early modern period. The reading is preceded by a brief discussion of the emergence of that ideologeme,
a historical account of the process by which in "the second half
of the Middle Ages (thirteenth to fifteenth centuries)...thought
based on the sign replaced that based on the symbol"; the reading
is followed by more general discussion of how the genre of the
novel is a manifestation of the ideologeme of the sign.[11] In this
account, intertextuality (here, the blending of narrational and
citational modes of utterance) is one textual feature that reveals
the novel's participation in the ideologeme of the sign. In order to
convey how different a properly intertextual study is from a traditional examination of sources, I offer a below a brief analysis of
book 1 of *Paradise Lost* that strives to respect Kristeva's original
sense of the term *intertextuality*, even to the point of employing
her specialized technical vocabulary. As in the case of her analysis of *Jehan de Saintré*, this analysis does not aim principally to
cast light on Milton's poem, but to read Milton's text so as to
illuminate the semiotic space the poem inhabits.

Milton's poem might not seem at first blush to recommend
itself for such an intertextual analysis. For Kristeva the semiotic
practice of the sign emerged in the late Middle Ages and lasted
until "the epistemological break of the nineteenth/twentieth

centuries."[12] La Sale's 1456 novel, therefore, usefully illustrates the semiotic practice of the sign displacing that of the symbol, just as Mallarmé and Lautréamont reflect the epistemological break of the late nineteenth century in Kristeva's *Revolution in Poetic Language*. But historically *Paradise Lost* sits squarely within the ideologeme of the sign, so defined. Given the broad strokes with which this semiotic history is painted, we might anticipate that Milton's poem would merely replay semiotic principles that the analysis of *Jehan de Saintré* brings to light, as in some measure it does. For instance, the revelation in the poem's opening line of the outcome of its story parallels the thematic closure Kristeva highlights in La Sale's novel. Likewise, the status of the poem's narrator as an agent among others in the story and the manner in which he merges his discourse with that of others (his muse, Moses, classical writers)—these features of *Paradise Lost* replay the *acteur-auteur* dynamic to which Kristeva calls attention in *Jehan de Saintré*.[13]

If the date of composition of *Paradise Lost* prevents an analysis of the poem from contributing much to a Kristevan semiotics, however, its genre complicates her epochal categories in a way that may yet make such an analysis fruitful. For the genre of epic is consistently invoked by Kristeva as belonging to the ideologeme of the symbol, rather than that of the sign. Perhaps Milton's poem, historically positioned within the ideologeme of the sign but generically affiliated with the ideologeme of the symbol, might recommend itself for a revealing intertextual analysis on those grounds.

One must be cautious, however, in undertaking such an analysis. As Jonathan Culler warns, intertextuality "is a difficult concept to use because of the vast and undefined discursive space it designates, but when one narrows it so as to make it more usable one either falls into source study of a traditional and positivistic kind (which is what the concept was designed to transcend) or else ends by naming particular texts as the pre-texts on the grounds of interpretive convenience." In warning us of these two traps,

Culler has, I believe, failed to recognize (and fallen into) a third. His error, which involves his use of the word *pre-texts,* may be made clear by examining his definition of that difficult concept, *intertextuality:* "Intertextuality thus becomes less a name for a work's relation to particular *prior* texts than a designation of its participation in the discursive *space* of a culture, the relationship between a text and the various languages or signifying practices of a culture and its relation to those texts which articulate for it the possibilities of that culture."[14] For Culler to speak of *pre*-texts, in the first passage I cited, might still suggest that intertextual analysis concerns itself with earlier works rather than with the "discursive space," contemporaneous with the text under consideration, that he properly emphasizes in the second.

I propose to address the difficulty Culler raises—that of selecting a text, on some grounds other than mere "interpretive convenience" from the "vast and undefined discursive space [intertextuality] designates"—by pushing to an extreme limit the notion of contemporaneity, the new historicists' "historical moment." One text that shares a strictly contemporaneous "discursive space" with *Paradise Lost* is an arithmetic textbook by James Hodder entitled *Hoder's Decimall Arithmatick.* The space they share is the page of the *Stationer's Register* for August 20, 1667; *Paradise Lost* is registered on that date. Beneath it, under the inscription *Eod die,* is registered Hodder's math textbook. Here is a text selected for comparison with *Paradise Lost* based neither on the premises of "source study of a traditional and positivistic kind" nor merely for "interpretive convenience," but rather on the grounds that it will allow an investigation of the synchronic discursive space within which Milton's epic found its conditions of intelligibility. On August 20, 1667, the printers for both John Milton and James Hodder assumed that the books for which they were seeking permission to publish could be construed as meaningful utterances given the various signifying practices operative within English culture at that moment.

It would be an enormous task to describe the innumerable semiotic resources on which these two texts draw in the process of elaborating their various significances. One would have to treat many obvious and banal presuppositions by which, even to this day, we make sense of math textbooks and epic poems—and distinguish between them. The "vast and undefined discursive space" which for Culler the term *intertextuality* designates would, he is right, be tedious to map in its entirety. I shall content myself with surveying only a few locales, semiotic territories occupied by both Hodder and Milton.

The full title of Hodder's text as it appears in the *Stationer's Register* is *Hoders Decimall Arithmatick; or, A Plainer and familior teaching the said Art, than hetherto hath beene published.* In the opening Hodder claims that he has "laboured to make a more clear discovery of some intricacies in this Art, than to my knowledge hath hitherto been."[15] For both this prefatory statement and the title to be comprehensible requires a semiotic order in which precedented/unprecedented functions as a signifying polarity. This same polarity, of course, is also part of what allows Milton's "Things unattempted yet in Prose or Rhime" to be construed as a significant utterance (and it is also, somewhat more subtly, at work in a passage like "thus they relate / Erring; for he with this rebellious rout / Fell long before") (*PL* 1.16, 746–48). In a culture that found no significance in whether or not a particular idea had been previously communicated, the force of such statements would not be felt. (We, of course, continue to find this distinction significant; we share this discursive space with Hodder and Milton, and so their claims continue, in a way that feels natural, to have meaning for us.) Because I am obviously not arguing that Milton appropriated this concept from Hodder (or vice versa), this brief example may help to suggest how intertextuality designates not so much a study of the relations *between texts* as a study of the semantic and cultural presuppositions that lie *between* two *texts* and allow both of them to have the meaning that they do.

A similar, but more complicated, instance of such intertextuality concerns the topic of education. In the early pages of *Hoders Decimall Arithmetick*, the stationer Thomas Rooks recommends the book on the basis that there are "very few of this kind yet set forth by any Teacher of this Art; and as I am informed those which are extant, of very little use to the *Learner*, without the help of an expert *Tutor*." The semantic polarity on which this statement would seem to depend for its meaning is one between self-instruction and instruction by someone more advanced in a given discipline. But Hodder's text is not aligned wholly with the former. Rooks goes on to reveal that he "delivered to several Professors and Students in this Art, Books of the former edition, desiring them to make their exceptions of what imperfection or obscurity they could find therein."[16] Thus, though one can use the book to teach oneself, the instruction in it is revealed to be ultimately that of "expert Tutors." The opposition between self-taught and tutored proves not so much a sharp either/or polarity as a *range* that makes significant a variety of intermediary positions.

As such, it exemplifies well one feature that for Kristeva distinguishes the ideologeme of the sign from that of the symbol: the principle of "non-disjunction." To return to Kristeva's broad semiotic history: in its vertical dimension, a symbol refers back to an "unrepresentable and unknowable universal transcendence"; "the symbol's function in its horizontal dimension (the articulation of signifying units among themselves) is one of escaping paradox; one could even say that the symbol is horizontally *antiparadoxical*: within its logic, two opposing units are exclusive. The good and the bad are incompatible—as are the raw and the cooked, honey and ashes, etcetera."[17] Signs differ from symbols in both of these dimensions of signification that Kristeva posits, both the vertical and horizontal dimensions. In the vertical dimension, instead of referring to a transcendental signified, both signified and signifier are "located on this side of the 'real' and 'concrete'"; in the horizontal dimension, signs do not exhibit the exclusive disjunction of symbols but are joined in a "network of multiple and always possible deviation."[18] Thus a "metonymical concatenation of deviations" link seeming opposites—here, self-taught/tutored.

There is an instance of this self-taught/tutored opposition (what Kristeva calls a "sememe") in Milton's epic: his portrayal of his instruction by the muse. And to examine Milton's version of this sememe is to see how *Paradise Lost* can complicate the semiotic history Kristeva sketches in "The Bounded Text." Milton's muse is the ultimate tutor; as the *agent* of Creation, it can, one assumes, inform him with perfect accuracy concerning anything therein. Nevertheless, Milton implicitly claims a unique relation to that tutor: if men (from whose ways, he will later tell us, he is "cut off") need him to justify God's ways to them, it is presumably because they cannot establish the particular type of relation with the Spirit that he has. Though he acknowledges being instructed by another, he nevertheless presents himself as somehow specially qualified to pass that instruction on. Here, then, we have a different "concatenation of deviations" than in Hodder's textbook, but it lies between the same semantic poles that were operative there.

Signification operates in both cases then, as Kristeva's principle of "non-disjunction" under the ideologeme of the sign would suggest. But Milton's invocation of the Muse does more than simply confirm the validity of Kristeva's semiotics. I will argue that through his portrayal of his muse, Milton actually manages to suggest, from within the ideologeme of the sign, the transcendence that for Kristeva is more characteristic of the ideologeme of the symbol—and not merely through some regression to an outmoded ideologeme, but by pushing to its very limits the reigning semiotic practice of his day in order to suggest a transcendence which that practice generally occludes.

Kristeva's ideologeme of the sign, as we have seen, operates through a series of deviations or exchanges that link semiotic elements, "both located on this side of the 'real.'" Therefore, as the classical "Heavenly Muse" of line 6 is replaced by (or specified to be) the Spirit of Oreb or Sinai, that very possibility of substitution would tend to suggest that the latter is no more transcendent than the former. But the substitutions continue and accelerate. The spirit of Oreb is replaced by that of Sion, then by the Christian Holy Spirit that prefers "before all temples th'upright heart and pure." Continuing on through the invocation, the phrase "thou from the first wast present" echoes a Homeric invocation and thus briefly suggests a return of the classical muse, but this muse immediately becomes the dovelike Christian Holy Spirit again, who is also the female (brooding) or male (impregnating) agent of Creation. The substitutions are so rapid and overwhelming that they here do not simply function according to the semiotic practice of the ideologeme of the sign, but do so flagrantly, calling attention to that operation so as to cast it into relief and utterly exhaust it, ultimately suggesting that some transcendence must underlie this storm of substitutions.

Literary critics following Boileau will refer to this dynamic (moving through an overwhelming profusion of data to an intuition of the transcendental) as the sublime—and count Milton as the great literary exemplar of sublimity. Within the broad strokes of Kristevan literary semiotics, the Miltonic sublime might be understood as reconstituting from within the ideologeme of the sign the sense of transcendence characteristic of the ideologeme of the symbol.

If this brief attempt to consider *Paradise Lost* in the spirit of Kristeva's original understanding of *intertextuality* illustrates nothing else, I trust that it illustrates the centrality of synchronism in critical projects like hers (even if her historical "moments" are epochal in scale). Such synchronism has been an important dimension of the approach to textual interrelations in poststructuralism generally and has perhaps been especially characteristic of the new historicism and cultural studies that have come to dominate literary scholarship since the 1980s (although critics now more typically use Foucauldian terms such as *discourse* or *discursive formation* than either of Kristeva's terms, *intertextuality* or *transposition*, to describe the semiotic practices in effect in a particular culture at a particular historical moment). Louis Montrose, for example, influentially characterized the (then) new historicism in precisely these terms, as a project that "reorients the axis of intertextuality, substituting for the diachronic text of an autonomous literary history the synchronic text of a cultural system."[19] (He uses the term *intertextuality* in its broader sense, rather than the strictly Kristevan sense.)

The term *intertextuality* itself (as the quotation from Montrose indicates) cannot by this point be limited to its original sense. The widespread looser application of the term testifies to, and results from, needs (that predated Kristeva's essays) of critics focused even on diachronic textual interrelations, traditionally understood. First, scholars of such textual relationships in some cases needed a term that describes a quality disseminated throughout the entirety of a text. The terms *allusion* or *verbal echo* name a brief, localized phenomenon. But some authors—Pope, Gray, Eliot, and Pound, for example, and perhaps above all, Milton—write poems so densely allusive that one wants a term to capture the frequency, the ubiquity even, of verbal echoes within their works. *Allusiveness* is awkward; but *intertextuality* seems to convey precisely this saturation of one text by phrases from the entire preceding literary tradition. A second reason for the misappropriation of the term *intertextuality* may be that many of the terms traditionally used in the analysis of interpoetic relationships often suggest an inequality between the two texts in question. Such terms as *source, borrowing,* and *echo* can suggest that the allusive text is of lesser stature than the text being evoked through allusion. The terminology can give the impression that the earlier text is possessed of an admirable creative plenitude, while the later text is secondary not just in time but also in value—derivative, unoriginal. The term *intertextuality,* by contrast, implies a relationship between equals and may on that basis be preferred over traditional terms by critics who wish to stress the later author's creativity in adapting the echoed phrases to a new context.

Even though the kind of analysis she intended to foster by coining the term *intertextuality* is significantly different from previous approaches to the relations between literary works, since even Kristeva herself abandoned the term, my first terminological resolution for the study that follows will be to concede to usage and employ *intertextuality* in the broadest way, to refer to all possible forms of textual interrelationship—though, where the distinction would be valuable, I will specify that I am focused on either *diachronic* or *synchronic* intertextuality.

Allusion, Echo

Diachronic intertextuality can, of course, take a number of forms: parody, cento, the strategies by which a work establishes itself within a particular genre or tradition, the direct answering by which works such as Marlowe's "Nymph's Reply to the Shepherd" respond to some antecedent literary work. The particular instances of diachronic intertextuality under consideration in this book—textual snippets reminiscent of a phrase in some earlier author's writing but smoothly incorporated into the new context of the imitating author's work—are distinguishable primarily by their being brief, discrete, and localized. While such phraseological adaptations may contribute to the total meaning or effect of the literary work in which they appear, due to their brevity, their impact (especially within larger works) is often localized, offering a subtle nuance of reinforcement or qualification of the phrase in which they are manifested or the immediate context in which they appear. In the council of devils that opens book 2 of *Paradise Lost*, Belial is described as someone whose "Tongue / Dropped Manna," a description that recalls Homer's description of Nestor "from whose lips the streams of words ran sweeter than honey" (*PL* 2.112–13; *Iliad* 1.239). Depending on the meaning that a particular reader assigns to this echo, the significance could conceivably ramify and bear on the entirety of *Paradise Lost,* but the allusion has its primary impact in its immediate context, presumably prompting the reader to compare the rhetorical power (but contrast the virtue) of Belial and Nestor. The two terms generally used to name these recontextualized phraseological imitations are, as I have mentioned, *allusion* and *verbal echo.* Neither term is entirely felicitous, as I shall show. The semantic range of the former is too broad, while that of the latter is too narrow.

Critics use the term *allusion* to name two phenomena that, while similar in some respects, are ultimately distinct. If a poet makes a reference to a little-known fact, or makes a roundabout reference to a well-known fact, we speak of this as an allusion. But we also use the term *allusion* for a poet's incorporation into his or her own poetry of a short phrase reminiscent of some phrase from an earlier work of literature. In the opening of *Paradise Lost,* the phrase "That Shepherd, who first taught the chosen Seed" is the first kind of allusion, a roundabout way of referring to the person of Moses; the phrase that follows, "In the beginning" is the second kind of allusion: incorporation of words from the opening of *Genesis* into Milton's poem (8–9).

These two types of allusion, learned or indirect reference and phraseological adaptation, differ significantly from one another, as I shall show more fully in a moment. But the two tend to be conflated under a single term for a number of reasons. One is that there is a species of allusion that combines aspects of the two phenomena: namely, indirect reference to an author or literary work. When Milton refers to Maeonides, that can be called an allusion (in the sense of a learned reference) to Homer—Homer the person, that is, not "Homer" as a designation for a particular collection of texts (3.35). Similarly, the proem to book 9 of *Paradise Lost* speaks of "*Neptune's* ire…that so long / Perplex'd the *Greek,*" a roundabout way of summarizing the plot of the *Odyssey* (18–19). One might call that too an allusion to Homer. But in both cases, one would be using the term very differently than when one observes, for example, that the phrase describing Mulciber's fall, "from Morn / to Noon he fell, from Noon to dewy Eve," alludes to Homer's description of Odysseus's slumber: "I slept nightlong, and into the dawn, and on to the noonday" (*Odyssey* 7.288; *PL* 1.742–43). The first two are simply circumlocutions that reference Homer or his works, while in the third case, Milton's very language is crafted on the model of a Homeric phrase.[20]

Another similarity between the two phenomena that go by the name of *allusion*—indirect or learned reference and phraseological adaptation—is that both may require scholarly annotation; and this points to more general similarities. Both are instances of what might be called advanced literacy. Moreover, the literacy that is necessary for the recognition of both learned references and phraseological adaptations is part of a larger precondition for recognizing either type of allusion, namely, that the reader must share a tradition with the author. (In fact, one of the effects of allusion, intended or not, is to divide an audience into those who have a cultural kinship with the author and those who do not.) In the case of a learned reference, this shared tradition takes the form of a body of knowledge with which both poet and reader are acquainted. In the case of phraseological adaptation, the nature of this shared tradition is a little more complex. Author and reader must have been exposed to the same text, which requires that the text be highly valued by both the author's and the reader's cultures—valued, moreover, in a way that encourages minute attention to verbal detail and mnemonic retention of such detail.

But despite these similarities, to incorporate a snippet of someone else's language into the flow of one's own is a significantly different matter than simply to refer in a learned or roundabout way. To begin to suggest the difference, we may consider a practical matter: what happens when a reader does not recognize each kind of allusion? Readers who do not know the information to which a learned reference or circumlocution alludes are generally aware of their ignorance ("I've never heard of Maeonides," "I don't know who 'that first Shepherd' is") and can often remedy it by consulting a reference source.[21] A phraseological adaptation is generally integrated unobtrusively into the alluding text, so that by contrast with a learned allusion, uninformed readers will generally not even be aware that they are missing anything; they will simply take the phrase as the later author's own. Milton's description of Satan's falling—"So Satan fell"—will make sense even to a reader unacquainted with Spenser.

The fact that a phraseological appropriation can be "covert," then, the fact that its derivation can go unnoticed, distinguishes it from learned or indirect reference, where, if the referent is unknown, a reader tends to be aware that he or she is missing something; and this practical difference points to a more essential difference between the two phenomena conflated under the term *allusion*. All language is referential, so learned or indirect references, though perhaps more obscure than other words in a poem, are not essentially different from them. While it is true that phraseological adaptations also often have a referential aspect, more immediately striking is their qualitative, almost ontological, difference from other language in a poem. An integrated verbal repetition treats preexisting phraseology almost as a sort of physical raw material that can be cut, reworked, and incorporated into a new setting—like scraps of paper glued to a collage or fragments of stone set into a mosaic. Pasco's preferred term, *graft*, highlights the almost physical quality of this phenomenon.

A phraseological appropriation calls attention not only to the expressive capacity, but also to the material nature of language. Part of the power of T. S. Eliot's line in "The Love Song of J. Alfred Prufrock," "I am not Prince Hamlet, nor was meant to be," resides in the strain between two different enunciations of the phrase "to be": the more vigorous emphasis provided by the rising intonation of Hamlet's question "to be or not to be," versus the deflated, prosaic intonation the phrase receives as part of Prufrock's quotidian declarative phrase, "meant to be."

This distinction between adaptation and reference has further implications. Because of the material nature of recontextualized phraseological adaptations, because the incorporated fragment has been almost visibly excised from its original situation, words *omitted* from the adopted phrase can come to be seen as significant, in a way for which there is no equivalent with learned references. Consider the previous example. Eliot's line contains both a reference (admittedly not especially learned or indirect) to the character of Hamlet and an echo of the phrase "to be or not to be." The reference to Hamlet may bring to mind any number of associations with that character that might bear on "The Love Song of J. Alfred Prufrock" (the protagonist's indecisiveness, his self-recriminations, his relations to women, and so on). But the echo works somewhat differently. For Eliot to echo only one-half of Hamlet's famous question calls attention to the omitted half, "or not to be"; perhaps Eliot thereby suggests that among the ways in which Prufrock is not like Prince Hamlet is his inability to contemplate a meaningful or heroic suicide.

Whatever meaning we may assign to the omission, we realize that no similar interpretation can be made of the reference, for there is no way in which the reference can emphasize a dimension of Hamlet's character as being deliberately excluded and thereby signify by omission. When Milton asks, "Who first seduc'd them to that foul revolt?" he, like Eliot, makes use of the capacity of echoes to signify by virtue of a deliberately omitted portion of a phrase (*PL* 1.33). His line echoes one from the *Iliad* in which Homer asks who set Achilles and Agamemnon at odds with one another: "Who among the gods set them in bitter contention?" (1.8). In his recasting of the line, Milton's omission of the Homeric phrase "among the gods" is perhaps intended to signal the recent loss of heavenly status in the figure to whom his question refers. Phraseological adaptations, then, unlike references, can signify by omission.

So there are a number of important respects in which the two phenomena generally conflated under the term *allusion* differ from one another. True, there is a playfulness in each: indirect references are like a riddle or trivia question ("by what name is Maeonides more commonly known?"); phraseological adaptations are like a sophisticated version of peek-a-boo or *fort-da*, in which some treasured object, having disappeared from immediate apperception, delightfully reemerges. This playfulness makes *allusion*, with its root of *ludo*, an appropriate term for the broad category. But it is also useful to keep in mind the differences between the two species of allusion and to have a set of terms for distinguishing them, when necessary.

Echo might seem an appropriate term to specify the type of allusion that I have been calling phraseological imitation or appropriation or adaptation. The term *echo* is already in common usage and, like Pasco's *graft*, it does have the advantage of calling attention to the physical quality of this kind of recontextualized verbal snippet. It must be used with some care, though, because if *allusion* is too broad a term to designate phraseological adaptations, *echo* can be too narrow. It is, at least, if it suggests that the prior text can be evoked only through a verbatim repetition of its phraseology. In some cases, it is true, an author will exactly duplicate an earlier author's phrase. In "To the Shade of Burns," Charlotte Smith speaks of Burns as one whom Great Nature taught to "build the lofty rhyme," an exact echo of the phrase from line 11 of *Lycidas*.[22] However, an author who recalls some earlier phrase will usually alter the adopted phrase—and not just its significance (which is almost inevitably modified as it is adapted to its new context), but generally even its phraseology. Much of the humor in Housman's "Malt does more than Milton can / To justify God's ways to man" results from the deflation of the grandiloquent "ways of God" to the colloquial "God's ways" as Housman shrinks Milton's pentameter to his own tetrameter.[23] Verbatim imitations, true echoes, are in fact more rare than adaptations that involve slight phraseological alterations.[24]

The slight imprecision of the word *echo* may seem a point hardly worth quibbling over. In critical parlance, after all, the term *echo* is obviously understood to indicate phrases that recall some earlier phrase, whether they do so through a verbatim repetition of that phrase or through some more general resemblance.

However, insofar as the word *echo* implies exact reduplication, it is one of those terms that tends to suggest that allusive texts are derivative and their authors unimaginative, and thus to diminish the accomplishment of allusive authors and the prestige of allusion study. For if the broader definition of the term is not kept in mind, then phrases such as "Milton echoes Homer" may give the impression not of a playful and creative adaptation of a precursor's language, but of a mechanical or slavish reiteration.

My second terminological proposal concerns the words *allusion* and *echo*. As is the case with *intertextuality*, these two terms are already so widely used within critical parlance to designate cases where some snippet of an earlier author's work is excised, refashioned, and recontextualized within the writing of some later author that it hardly seems worthwhile to propose an alternative term, particularly something cumbersome like *phraseological appropriation* or *adaptation*. Nevertheless, I will use the terms *allusion* and *echo*, mindful of their inadequacy, and will employ the more exact *phraseological adaptation* and *learned circumlocution* when a more precise distinction is desirable.

Spur, Reprise

Some further consideration of the term *echo* may point to another terminological deficiency that plagues the study of phraseological adaptations. The phenomenon is bipartite in nature: phrase X in the work of some later author recalls phrase Y in the writing of some earlier author. It would be useful to have a set of distinguishing terms for the two phrases (and a third term still for the entire dyad). If the later phrase is called an *echo*, how are we to refer to the earlier phrase? What is the name for the initial sounding that generates an echo? A *call*? A *cry*? Those do not seem entirely felicitous terms for the phrase on which an echo is modeled. Nor is the word *source* entirely appropriate, since it generally names the entire work in which the imitated phrase appears (an objection that applies to *subtext* as well). The absence of a simple term that might be paired with *echo* to designate the earlier phrase on which the adaptation is based reveals a significant limitation in the technical vocabulary available for analyzing the phenomenon.

Compounding this confusion is the fact that in critical parlance the term *allusion* sometimes serves to designate the imitative phrase alone and sometimes the entire double unit of imitative and imitated phrases. Consider, for example, John K. Hale's treatment of the Miltonic phrase, "If thou beest he, but oh how fallen! How changed." He notes that this recalls Virgil's "quantum mutatos ab illo" and says of the Miltonic phrase, "many readers have found here an allusion to the shock with which Virgil's Aeneas meets the ghost of his kinsman Hector."[25] Hale's "here" is presumably to be understood as meaning "in this phrase from *Paradise Lost*," so what is meant by the term *allusion* must be Milton's phrase specifically, a fact that is confirmed when Hale begins a question with "even if it does allude," where "it" must be understood as the Miltonic phrase specifically. A moment later, however, Hale uses the term *allusion* for the entire double unit of Miltonic and Virgilian phrases; when he says "in short, the allusion enables Milton to implant several pertinent things at once in the responsive reader," the term *allusion* must here refer to the Miltonic phrase *in combination with* the Virgilian phrase (and those elements of the Virgilian context that enrich the meaning of the Miltonic phrase). In context, Hale's meaning is clear enough. But it cannot be conducive to clarity, particularly in general discussion of the phenomenon, to have one word name both the whole entity *and* one of its parts.

The situation is almost exactly analogous to the one that prompted I. A. Richards to coin the terms *tenor* and *vehicle* in order to be able to separate out, for critical discussion, elements of a metaphor: "one of the oddest of the many odd things about the whole topic," Richards observed, "is that we have no agreed distinguishing terms for [the] two halves of a metaphor—in spite of the immense convenience, almost the necessity of such terms if we are to make any analyses without confusion." In Richards's case, he notes that the term *metaphor* is "sometimes used for the whole double unit" and "sometimes for one of its two components [the one he calls the *vehicle*] in separation from the other."[26] In just this way *allusion* is sometimes used to refer to the whole double unit of imitative and imitated phrase, and sometimes used for just one of its components: the imitative phrase alone.

The terms that critics have proposed to designate specifically the imitative phrase have not been especially felicitous. Ziva Ben-Porat speaks of a "sign containing a *marker*" that brings about the "simultaneous activation of two texts"; Garner speaks of a "trigger."[27] These terms do highlight the function of the imitative phrase in calling to mind the phrase on which it is modeled, thereby inviting a hermeneutic process of comparing the allusive text to the evoked text. But terms such as *trigger* and *activation*—besides suggesting, wrongly, that imitative phrases inevitably call to mind the phrases on which they are based—also give a rather reductive and mechanistic impression of how a reminiscence operates (only slightly softened by Alter's use of *signal* in place of *marker* or *trigger*). Moreover, by suggesting that the imitative phrase is purely functional, directing us to the prior text in a search for details that might enrich the meaning of the allusive text, the term *trigger* is yet one more phrase that subtly suggests the derivative, secondary status of the later author relative to the (original, plentiful) precursor. Finally, terminology such as that used by Ben-Porat, Garner, and Alter still leaves us with no term to designate the phrase in its initial incarnation.

This seems a situation analogous to the one in which Richards found himself, and one that may similarly warrant the introduction of new terminology. I propose that, in cases where it would be useful to be able to distinguish the phrase in the later author that recalls from the phrase in the earlier author that is recalled, we speak of the echo as a *reprise* and the initial version of the phrase as a *spur*. The initial phrase is a spur both in the sense that, like a rock spur, it somehow *stuck out* to the alluding author and in the sense that, like an equestrian's spur, it *provided an impetus* for his or her allusive reappropriation. And a reprise is a taking-up-again, which is exactly what the later author does with the earlier phrase. This pair of terms is intended to stress the creativity of the adapting author as well as the one whose phraseology is adapted. If anything, I hope that the pair slightly privileges the agency of the later author by stressing what he or she does with the stimulus that the earlier author provided, and that it might thus gently counteract the tendency of terms such as *echo, borrowing,* or *influence* to suggest a secondary, lesser, or derivative status for the imitating author. A spur may provide an impetus for the alluding author, but the reprise represents what he or she makes of that prompting. Using the proposed terminology, then, we would say that Milton's description of Satan's fall in *Paradise Lost* is an allusion to (in the specific sense of a phraseological adaptation of) Spenser's description of the dragon's fall in book 1 of the *Faerie Queene*. In particular, the reprise "So Satan fell" has as its spur the Spenserian phrase "So downe he fell."

One final clarification is in order before we turn to consider the variety of uses to which phraseological adaptations may be put and how the analysis of diachronic allusion and synchronic intertextuality might be coordinated. When dealing with long works, one further conceptual and terminological difficulty arises. The signifying impact of an allusion is, as I have mentioned, often localized. As Ben-Porat schematizes it (but using the terminology I have been proposing), when a knowledgeable reader encounters a reprise, it sends him or her back (in memory, at least) to the spur.[28] The reader considers whether any elements of the spur bear on the allusive text in such a way as to enrich or qualify its meaning. For shorter texts, this is indeed the basic process. But a single reprise might not "activate" the entirety of a lengthy evoked text; it may evoke primarily the immediate context of the spur. Moloch's speech in book 2 of *Paradise Lost* — "His utmost ire...will either quite consume us...or...we are at worst on this side nothing" — recalls one made by Ajax in the fifteenth book of the *Iliad,* when the Trojans are nearing the Greek ships: "Better to take in a single time our chances of dying or living than go on being squeezed in the stark encounter right up against the ships" (*PL* 2.95–101; *Iliad* 15.511–13). In such cases, I will use the word *passage* or the phrase *immediate context* in a quasi-technical way to refer to the text immediately surrounding either the spur or the reprise and reserve the word *source* or *subtext* for the entire larger work in which the spur appears. In this case, then, we would say that Milton's reprise sends readers back to the immediate context of the spur in Homer's account, inviting them to consider whether any elements of that passage enrich or qualify the immediate context of that reprise in *Paradise Lost.* Ajax's courage here helps to emphasize Moloch's annihilation-defying resolve. Together, the numerous allusions to the *Iliad* in *Paradise Lost* evoke the whole of Homer's epic as a subtext in order to mark the difference between Milton's vision and Homer's. But individual reprises may recall particular smaller portions of the *Iliad* and *Odyssey* for more specific local purposes.

Functions and Effects of Allusion

Most studies of allusion are resolutely hermeneutic in orientation. One critic explicitly describes allusions that do not contribute to a text's meaning as "inherently uninteresting"; most others simply assume that the hermeneutic dimension of allusion is the only one worth studying.[29] Edward Stein says, "It seems to me...necessary to require that the truly allusive marker, in inviting construal entrain a manifest enrichment of connotation in the alluding text"; and so strong is this assumption that he speaks of echoes that do not do so as "non-allusive" echoes.[30] William Porter has built an entire taxonomy of "literary associations"—running from appropriation, through reminiscence, echo, and borrowing, to critical allusion—based on how much the echoed passage enriches the meaning of the echoing one—but labeling all types other than critical allusion as "lesser forms of literary intertextuality."[31]

One deleterious effect of this focus on meaning has been to mire the theory of allusion in irresolvable issues of intentionality. Another has been that commentators on allusion have neglected the fact that enriching or qualifying local significance is not the only effect that allusions can have nor the only purpose they can serve. Allusions can help to establish a work's genre. Through an allusion, an author can signal an affiliation—literary, political, or personal. Allusions serve to establish a work's implied audience. The "fit audience" that Milton wants Urania to find for his epic is clearly one with a broad knowledge of the Western intellectual and literary tradition. By contrast, the obscurity of some of the allusions in Eliot's *The Waste Land* demands scholarly annotation—which Eliot, in part, himself provides—and the allusions thereby signal that the modern age has lamentably lost a common literary culture and tradition. Allusions may establish a feeling of rapport between author and reader. Certain aspects of how they function—that they exercise the memory, for instance—may even in particular cases be important. Milton, for example, associates the Fall with a lapse in memory. In *Paradise Lost* he has Raphael warn Adam to "*remember* [the example of Satan] and fear to transgress"; and the narrator's assessment, after the Fall, of Adam and Eve's actions is that they "ought to have still *remember'd* / The high Injunction not to taste that Fruit" (6.912, 10.12–13; emphasis mine). Given the importance that Milton attaches to memory, perhaps the allusive density of *Paradise Lost* is not merely an accident of his vast learning; perhaps the allusions are designed to offer the reader the opportunity to exercise a mental faculty that Milton regarded as essential to moral decision making. A number of the chapters in this study will attempt to offer a richer sense of the possible effects allusion can have or uses to which it can be put. In chapter 2, for example, I note that allusions always possess an evaluative dimension; in chapter 3 I argue that the mere quality of familiarity can have a function within allusive language. And the book as a whole seeks to illustrate the role that intertextuality plays in establishing a particular work in the literary canon.

Beyond broadening our understanding of the effects to which allusive language can be put, though, the most important theoretical initiative of this study will be to coordinate allusion more fully with the synchronic intertextualities that have characterized poststructuralist literary criticism. Although it is understandable that early poststructuralist critics felt a need, in setting out their theoretical premises, to distinguish their approaches from traditional forms of literary study, the diachronic intertextuality of allusion is not, as critics like Culler and Montrose have suggested, antithetical to synchronic considerations of a text in its particular historical moment. Indeed, in the next section, I will argue that just as the study of allusion stands to benefit from the insights of post structuralism and new historicism, those forms of criticism can in turn be enriched by a more sophisticated consideration of the phenomenon of allusion; the preconditions involved in readers noticing allusions, and which guide their interpretation of allusions, illuminate the cultural circumstances of those readers. Allusions to earlier authors are no less "cultural" a phenomenon than the relations between literary texts and such things as sumptuary laws, accounts of the colonial enterprise, medical treatises, and the whole host of other contemporaneous texts in connection with which we have been reading literary works since the 1980s.

Homer à la Mode

Just two years before *Paradise Lost* was published, James Scudamore published what he called a "Mock Poem upon the First and Second Books of Homer's Iliads" titled *Homer à la Mode*.[32] Homer is rendered "à la mode" in Scudamore's parody in two senses. First, the characters and plot developments of Homer's epic are conveyed with seventeenth century equivalents. Chryses is likened to a sexton, Nestor to an alderman or keeper of a parish register; the Greek soldiers pray rosaries and say "Ave Marys."[33] The second sense in which Homer is made "à la mode" by Scudamore's poem is that the high seriousness of Homeric epic is converted to the ribaldry we regard as characteristic of Restoration literature. Achilles's sea-goddess mother Thetis catches crawfish "and often times had rid in state / And sate i' th' bottom of a poole / Inthroned in a cucking-stoole." To confirm his oath, Jove shakes Olympus not by the terrible nodding of his head, but "not being abl' his wind to containe / He let a f--- that shook the mountain."[34]

Scudamore's parodic refashioning of Homer is just a more overt and striking instance of a process of remaking canonical texts that goes on more subtly even in editions, translations, and commentaries that seek faithfully to reproduce older authors' works for modern audiences. Theorists of canonicity such as Barbara Herrnstein Smith and John Guillory stress that canonical works of literature do not simply persist through time, their intrinsic qualities recognized by successive generations of readers, but that each generation of readers reproduces the classic work in a modern guise.[35] Smith describes the nature of the reproduction of canonical works:

> the value of a literary work is continuously produced and reproduced by the very acts of implicit and explicit evaluation that are frequently invoked as "reflecting" its value and therefore as being evidence of it. In other words, what are commonly taken to be the signs of literary value are, in effect, also its *springs*. The endurance of a classic canonical author such as Homer, then, owes not to the alleged transcultural or universal value of his works, but, on the contrary, to the continuity of their circulation in a particular culture. Repeatedly cited and recited, taught and imitated, and thoroughly enmeshed in the network of intertextuality that continuously *constitutes* the high culture of the orthodoxly educated population of the West (and the Western-educated population of the rest of the world), that highly variable entity we refer to as "Homer" recurrently enters our experience in relation to a large number and variety of our interests and thus can perform a large number of various functions for us and obviously has performed them for many of us over a good bit of the history of our culture.[36]

Smith is contesting David Hume's claim that "the same Homer who pleased at Athens two thousand years ago is still admired at Paris and London." She insists it is not "the same Homer" who has endured through time, but a "highly variable entity we refer to as 'Homer,'" who has performed various functions, been understood and interpreted in various ways, in each of the geographically distinct and chronologically successive "particular cultures" that make up Western culture.

For what might serve as a particularly stark illustration of this principle, consider a version of Homer that appeared at the very time that Milton was composing *Paradise Lost*. In 1659, Thomas Grantham published a translation of book 1 of the *Iliad*. In 1660, he published a second edition of the translation. The two editions are identical except for their treatment of the first six lines of the poem. The 1659 translation begins with what I will call "version A" of those lines:

> Achilles Son of Pelus Goddess sing
> His banefull wrath which to the Greeks did bring
> Unnumbered griefs, brave souls to hell did send,
> Their noble bodies Fowls and dogs did rend;
> Iove will'd all this, he these to strife did bring,
> Godlike Achilles and Atreides King.

In the back of the book, he has a little note indicating that he had originally rendered the first six lines differently, and he provides the alternate translation, which I will refer to as "version B":

> Goddess the wrath of great Achilles sing,
> Who griefs unnumbred to the Greeks did bring,
> And many valiant souls to hell did send,
> Their noble bodies Fowls and Dogs did rend;
> Jove will'd all this, from him this strife begun,
> Of Agamemnon and great Pel'us son.

In the note, he claims that, after showing version B to many scholars, he found "one Gentleman something curious," and altered the opening passage to version A, which appears at the start of the 1659 edition.

Remarkably, when he published the second edition of his translation in 1660, Grantham reversed the two passages. The 1660 edition begins with version B. It has the same note at the end, but this time, claiming that he had shown version A to many scholars and because "one Gentleman [was] something curious," he opted for version B. The two claims cannot, of course, both be true; what, then, is going on here? One possible explanation for this curious reversal might be the Restoration itself. The most significant difference between the alternate passages concerns line 6. For contemporary readers, the phrasing of version A, "Godlike Achilles and Atreides King" (closer to the original, incidentally), might recall the recent civil wars, which had been cast (at least by the republicans) as a conflict between a "king" and the "godly" populace. In 1659, while England was still under the Commonwealth government, such a reference might have been permissible or even welcome, so Grantham printed version A. But with a restoration potentially in the offing, to cover himself he presented his choice as if it had been suggested by someone else. In 1660, he suppressed the line that suggests a painful and unwelcome analogy between the events of the *Iliad* and England's recent past. But in case the Restoration did not hold, he again provided himself an out: he only preferred this version because of the prompting of the curious gentleman.

Grantham's slipperiness here (if that is indeed what it is) registers the uncertainty English citizens must have felt regarding the significant political upheaval of this historical moment, as it approached and just after it occurred. Not always is there such a decisive, watershed difference between one era and another, but the point made starkly by Grantham's translations is, as literary criticism since the 1980s illustrates, more broadly true: the political and social milieu of a particular culture has a direct impact on the form cultural artefacts take. Homer is always "à la mode."

This study represents an effort to consider *Paradise Lost* in connection with Homer's epics as they were understood in Milton's day. David Norbrook's reading of Milton's allusions to Lucan, as Lucan was appropriated by mid-seventeenth-century republican authors, serves as a model for my study.[37] Although, as Norbrook implicitly notes, Homer was perhaps less politically charged than Virgil and Lucan, there was in fact in England, as later chapters will show, a flurry of Homeric activity in just the years during which *Paradise Lost* was being composed. In addition to Scudamore's parody, John Ogilby in 1660 brought out a new translation of the epics, the first since George Chapman's. And Zachary Bogan and James Duport brought out scholarly works on Homer in 1658 and 1660.

Because of the way in which certain poststructuralist terms and concepts emerged, in contrast with allusion as traditionally understood, I must emphasize that allusions to prior literary texts are no less "cultural" than synchronic intertextual connections; indeed, they are no less "synchronic." Whether a reader notices an allusion in the first place and how he or she interprets it once it has been noticed are matters determined by the political and cultural circumstances of that reader's particular historical moment.[38] The entire book is intended as an illustration of this principle, but let me briefly illustrate the impact that a reader's historical moment has on perceiving and interpreting an allusion by examining two of Milton's allusions, one to Virgil and one to Homer, and how these have been treated by various editors through the past three centuries.

In book 9 of *Paradise Lost*, when Eve returns after having eaten of the forbidden fruit, Adam's reaction is described as follows:

> On th'other side, *Adam*, soon as he heard
> The fatal Trespass don by Eve, amaz'd,
> Astonied stood and Blank, while horror chill
> Ran through his veins, and all his joynts relax'd;
> From his slack hand the Garland wreath'd for *Eve*
> Down drop'd and all the faded Roses shed:
> Speechless he stood and pale, till thus at length
> First to himself he inward silence broke.   (888–95)

Editors (beginning with Patrick Hume in 1695, and including Henry James Todd, Merritt Y. Hughes, and Alastair Fowler) have noted in this passage an allusion to a verse in the twelfth book of the *Aeneid*. In the penultimate line of Virgil's epic, just before the soul of Turnus famously "flees murmuring into the shades below," his bodily reaction to Aeneas's sword thrust is described as follows: "solvuntur frigore membra," his limbs dissolved with cold.[39] This phrase seems pretty clearly to have served as a model for Milton's "horror *chill* / Ran through his veins, and all his *joints relax'd.*"

However, neither Hume nor any other editor of Milton notes that this phrase — "solvuntur frigore membra" — occurs in another spot in Virgil's epic. In the first book of the *Aeneid*, when Aeneas sees the storm that Juno has stirred up, his limbs similarly dissolve with cold: "extemplo Aeneae solvuntur frigore membra" (1.92). What is odd about this editorial oversight is that the passage from book 1 of the *Aeneid* arguably represents a closer parallel to, and more likely model for, Milton's lines than does the passage from book 12. In both the passage from book 1 and the Miltonic passage, this description of the main character's bodily reaction precedes a speech; and in both cases, the speech is a despairing one spoken by the character to himself. Aeneas groans, "O, three and four times blessed / were those who died before their fathers' eyes / beneath the walls of Troy" (133–35). Furthermore, the word *extemplo*, "suddenly," which appears only in the book 1 version of the Virgilian phrase, has a parallel in Milton's "Soon as."

Now, my intent is not to argue that the passage from book 1 of the *Aeneid*, as opposed to the one in book 12, is the true source for Milton's phrasing. He might well have had both of the Virgilian passages in mind, since Adam's reaction to Eve's trespass — "with thee / Certain my resolution is to Die" — makes his fate here essentially equivalent to that of Turnus at the end of the *Aeneid*. Instead, I want to ask about this allusion the kind of question that the cultural criticism since the 1980s has encouraged us to ask: what happened between 1667 and 1695 that made Hume (and later editors) fail to notice, or elect not to mention, the model from book 1 of the *Aeneid* for this Miltonic passage?

Since we know so little about Patrick Hume, this question, asked with reference to biographical considerations, would have to be purely speculative. But of course I do not mean to ask the question in that way: rather, I am asking what happened *within literary culture at large* between 1667 and 1695 that might have inclined an editor to cite the passage from book 12 of the *Aeneid* as the model for Milton's phrasing, rather than the passage from book 1, which is at least equally likely to have served as Milton's source.

A number of developments in the latter half of the seventeenth century focused critical attention on book 12 of the *Aeneid*. First, and most simply, around 1650 editors stopped printing, as they had customarily done over the preceding 200 years, the so-called thirteenth book of the *Aeneid* by Maffeo Vegio and started stressing that the *Aeneid* was complete as Virgil had left it (in terms of narrative, that is; they continued to credit the account that Virgil had, when he died, still been in the process of refining his verses). The introductory matter of the edition by Charles de La Rue, for example (the edition that Dryden used in preparing his translation of the *Aeneid*), considering the Aristotelian premise that the action of an epic must be *complete*, explicitly dismisses Vegio's supplement as unnecessary; prophesies from earlier in the epic, La Rue claims, sketch out all that readers need to know about what will happen upon Turnus's death.[40]

These changes in editorial practice may have combined with elements of the emerging critical outlook of the later seventeenth century to incline a Miltonic editor like Hume toward the "solvuntur frigore membra" of book 12, rather than that of book 1.

In 1668, Rene Rapin published his *Comparaison des poems d'Homere et de Vergile*, a work that Samuel Monk regards as an important precursor to Boileau's highly influential 1674 *L'arte poetique* and translation of Longinus.[41] The *Comparaison* was translated into English in 1672. In his work, Rapin sets out a definition of the epic derived from Aristotle and Horace and then evaluates the epics of Homer and Virgil according to the elements of that definition, in their order of importance. He finds Virgil superior to Homer on the most important points. One area where Virgil surpasses Homer concerns the "unity of the subject and time of the two poems." According to Rapin, the *Iliad* should have ended with the death of Hector: "after the death of Hector, which ought to have clos'd the action, there are still two Books to come; the 23. which comprehends the Exercises celebrated for the death of Patroclus, and which contribute nothing to the principal action; and the 24. which contains the Lamentations of the Trojans, and the ransoming of Hector's body, which have no connection to the principal action, that being compleat without it." By contrast, Virgil ends his epic at just the right moment: "Does not the *Æneid* take its period much better by the death of *Turnus*, which closes the action? *Virgil* does not carry on things any further; he knew well enough that he had committed a fault if he had not stop'd there."[42]

Dryden's introductory dedication to his 1695 translation of the *Aeneid* similarly provides evidence that in the later seventeenth century critical attention was focused more on the concluding book than on the opening book of Virgil's epic. For example, in defending Aeneas's character, he claims that except for his grief for Pallas, Aeneas would "by his Natural Compasion" have forgiven Turnus, but then "the poem had been left imperfect: for then we could have had no certain prospect of his Happiness, while the last Obstacle to it was unremoved." In his consideration of the poem's divine machinery, Dryden also focuses on several developments in the twelfth book: Jove's tipping of the heavenly scales in favor of Aeneas, and his use of a Fury and screech owl to distract Turnus during his fatal combat with Aeneas.[43]

In short, given the critical preoccupations of the day, readers like Hume might simply have been looking more frequently and more closely at the final book of Virgil's epic than at its opening—and might therefore have remembered the phrase "solvuntur frigore membra" from book 12, rather than book 1. Alternately, in citing the phrase from book 12, Hume might deliberately have been steering clear of a passage that, it had been argued, brought discredit on Aeneas. The French critic living in exile in England, Charles de Saint-Evremond, cited *Aeneid* 1.92 as showing an absence in Aeneas of the heroic quality of valor.[44]

My concern here is not to determine indisputably the cause for Hume's oversight, but to make a point about allusion, a point that in some ways one ought not need to make, but because of how certain strains of poststructuralism defined themselves at their emergence, one must in fact make: that allusion is a cultural matter. Allusion is not a phenomenon the analysis of which presupposes a naïve belief (rendered obsolete by recent culturally oriented criticism) in what Montrose calls "the diachronic text of an autonomous literary history"; rather, as much as any other aspect of a text, the workings of allusion are a function of the cultural conditions that obtain within a particular historical moment. For a reader to notice an allusion presupposes a number of cultural conditions: a society that values literary texts, that makes efforts to preserve and disseminate them and to assign authorial "ownership" to selected passages within them; an educational system that encourages memorization and close attention to verbal detail; and so on.

And, of course, how a reader interprets an allusion once he or she has noticed it is, if anything, even more culturally determined. Consider Raphael's account, in book 5 of *Paradise Lost*, of the Father's begetting of the Son. After God has appointed him the head of all the angels, the celebration that ensues is described as follows:

> Eevning now approach'd
> (For wee have also our Eevning and our Morn,
> Wee ours for change delectable, not need)
> Forthwith from dance to sweet repast they turn
> Desirous; all in Circles as they stood,
> Tables are set, and on a sudden pil'd
> With Angels Food, and rubied Nectar flows:
> In Pearl, in Diamond, and massie gold,

Fruit of delicious Vines, the growth of Heav'n.
On flours repos'd, and with fresh flourets crownd,
They eate, they drink, and in communion sweet
Quaff immortalitie and joy, secure
Of surfet where full measure onely bounds
Excess, before th' all bounteous King, who showrd
With copious hand, rejoycing in thir joy.   (627–41)

All that having taken place, we are then told that, "ambrosial Night with Clouds exhal'd / From that high mount of God" (642–43). Milton's calling night "ambrosial" constitutes a phraseological adaptation of Homer, who in the second book of the *Iliad* speaks of ἀμβροσίην...νύκτα (57). (The words in the Homeric spur are the etymological roots of the words in the Miltonic reprise, so the allusion is a translinguistic echo.)

To suggest the impact of a reader's historical moment on that reader's interpretation of an allusion, I will examine how this echo has been glossed by editors in successive generations. In 1695, Milton's earliest editor, Patrick Hume, notes the Homeric spur and then glosses the phrase as follows: "Divine Night, from the pleasant refreshment and necessary support Sleep affords us. *Ambrosia* is used of the *Poetick* Food by which the Gods maintained their *Immortality*, thence us'd for sweet, delicious and invigorating."[45] Half a century later, in his 1749 edition, Thomas Newton also focuses on the alimentary meaning, but he omits Hume's reference to the way in which ambrosia sustains the immortality of divinities. Newton glosses as follows: "So Homer calls the night ambrosial...and sleep for the same reason ambrosial, because it refreshes and strengthens as much as food, as much as ambrosia."[46] Todd's variorum editions, beginning in 1801 and reprinted throughout the nineteenth century, simply reproduce Newton's note.[47] In his 1957 *Complete Poems and Major Prose*, Merritt Y. Hughes does not gloss the line at all. Fowler's edition of 1968 glosses "ambrosial" as "fragrant"; he notes the Homeric source, but then sends readers to an earlier gloss, the one for line 245 of book 2.[48] That note glosses "ambrosial" in a way that gives priority to the olfactory meaning, noting first that "ambrosial" means "fragrant and perfumed," mentioning that it can also mean "immortal," because "ambrosia was the fabled food, or drink, of the gods," but then going on to reiterate the olfactory meaning by noting, "It was, however, also identified by the herbalist with certain specific plants; see, e.g. Gerard, *Herball* (1597) p. 950: 'The fragrant smell that this kind of Ambrosia or Oke of Cappadocia [sometimes 'Oak of Jerusalem'] yeeldeth, hath mooved the Poets to suppose that this herbe was the meate and foode for the gods.'"[49] Roy Flannagan in 1998 omits any reference to Homer and focuses entirely on the olfactory significance: "The night is fragrant, since it is perfumed with clouds exhaled from the Mount of God."[50]

Obviously each individual editor will bring to the task of annotation his or her own personal interpretive insights and preferences. But the way in which each of these editors glosses the phrase "ambrosial night" is also at least partly a function of cultural presuppositions at work in each editor's historical moment, and in particular presuppositions related to the way in which Homer was constructed in each century. For if allusions to Homer (and other earlier authors) are not properly placed on some diachronic axis of intertextuality, but are, as I am claiming, as synchronically "cultural" a matter as the contemporaneous texts in connection with which we now read literary works, that is because, as theorists of canon formation have insisted, canonical authors do not simply persist through time but are variably reproduced by each generation of readers and critics.

For Hume, as for many in the seventeenth century, heathen poets like Homer see the truths revealed to Christians "as through a glass darkly." In fact, they derive their descriptions of supernatural phenomena ultimately from the Hebraic Scriptures: "That the Mosaical Philosophy is the most ancient, is not only very certain, but [it is also certain] that all the Heathen Poets, and their greatest philosophers too, borrowed their Description of the Chaos, and what they delivered of the first Formation of Matter from the Creation as delineated by Moses, whose writings many of them saw, though they did not understand them."[51] Despite their incomplete comprehension of Moses, but perhaps because of their derivation from him, Homer and other ancient poets are regarded as usefully supplementing the account of supernatural phenomena provided in the Scriptures. So, for example, in glossing "the void profound of unessential night," Hume notes, "Night was by the Ancients esteemed a goddess, or rather the Mother of all the Gods, as being before the creation of any thing, Darkness approaching nearest to, and being the best resemblance of, Non-entity."[52] Hume's gloss on "ambrosial night" also seems to work in this way; for Hume, Homer suggests an angelological fact not directly revealed in Scripture: that the angels sustain their immortality in part through the refreshment that heavenly night provides, which they take in almost like a kind of food.

When we turn to Newton, we see him backing away from any supernatural significance in the phrase "ambrosial night." Night "refreshes and strengthens as much as food," he says, adding (because it is the part of the line that needs the gloss, but seemingly as an afterthought), "as much as ambrosia." Newton's gloss is in keeping with the more rationalistic ethos of the eighteenth century, and also with the increasingly rationalistic construction of Homer during that period. As Howard Clarke remarks, Alexander Pope is a transitional figure: "the last of Homer's commentators to make full use of the allegorical tradition," he was nevertheless "plainly uncomfortable" with its "fine-spun interpretations."[53] Even before his translations of Homer's epics, as early as his *Essay on Criticism*, Pope was casting Homer less as a source for knowledge about the supernatural than as the poet who had best expressed the laws of the natural world. When "t'examine ev'ry part" Virgil came, "*Nature* and *Homer* were, he found, the *same*."[54]

As we move into the twentieth century, Homer tends to be constructed less as an author whose lines provide valuable information about either the supernatural world (as they did for Hume) or the natural world (as they did for Newton and Pope), and more as a generic exemplar.[55] Flannagan's introduction to *Paradise Lost* in the *Riverside Milton*, for example, begins with a section entitled "A Short History of the Epic Genre." He claims, "For Milton, the word [*epic*] would have meant the noblest works of Homer, Vergil, Dante, Boiardo, Tasso, Spenser...writing in their most expansive genre." And conversely, the word *Homer* in Flannagan's presentation, would have meant primarily a genre: "In western European literature, the epic genre begins with Homer's *Iliad* and *Odyssey*."[56] Given late twentieth century construction of Homer primarily as a generic exemplar (and our reading of him primarily in translation, which is a related issue), it is not entirely surprising that Fowler deemphasizes the Homeric derivation in favor of a meaning of "fragrant," that Flannagan chooses not to mention the Homeric spur, and that Hughes chooses not to gloss this passage at all. After all, Homer's calling night "ambrosial" is no part of the construction of an epic poem (especially given "ambrosial night" is not a repeated phrase, like "rosy-fingered dawn" and thus not strikingly part of the oral-formulaic composition of Homer's primary epic). "Ambrosial night" is just an intriguing thing that Homer said in the course of his poem, and since Homer does not exist for us primarily as a source of information about the natural or supernatural world, the Homeric spur for "ambrosial night" is not worthy of notice within our historical moment.[57]

Whether a reader discerns a particular spur behind a given allusive reprise, then, and how he or she interprets the allusion once it has been noticed, are matters strongly affected by larger cultural determinants: the evoked text's preservation in available archives, its dissemination through various forms of publication, whether and how it is taught within the educational system, the kind of critical commentary it generates, and so on. The interpretation of allusions, therefore, should be sensitive to historical difference in such matters. Ultimately, it is not enough simply to note that phrase *X* in one author recalls phrase *Y* in a precursor (though critical editions admittedly only have space for such identifications).

To understand what an author may have intended by a particular allusion, where possible one should try to establish how the
source text in general, and the spur behind a given reprise in particular, were understood in the alluding author's day.

Let us return to the passage in book 9, in which, on Eve's return
to Adam, "horror chill / Ran through his veins and all his joynts
relax'd." Whichever of the two Virgilian spurs Milton may have
had in mind when he composed his lines, he would have been
aware that those Virgilian passages were themselves modeled
on verses from Homer. Three times in the *Odyssey* we are told
that Odysseus's knees went slack, καὶ τότ' Ὀδυσσῆος λύτο γούνατα
(5.297, 406; 22.147). The first of these is probably the most immediate model for the passage in book 1 of the *Aeneid*, for it is
spoken during a storm at sea and precedes a speech of Odysseus
which, like that of Aeneas, describes as "three and four times
happy those Danaans were who died then / In wide Troy land"
(5.306–07). As in the case of its Virgilian and Miltonic remakings,
the Homeric spur precedes a despairing speech spoken by a character to himself.

But in fact Milton might have yet another instance of Homeric
knee-slackening in mind when he describes Adam's reaction to
Eve's return. In a critical treatise on Homer, attributed in Milton's
day to Plutarch and appended to many editions of the Homeric
epics, the critic, admiring Homer's skill in the depiction of
human passions, adduces a pair of passages to illustrate "the difference between the moderate man [and the immoderate man]."[58]
The two passages contrast the reactions to Penelope of Odysseus
and of the suitors. Pseudo-Plutarch remarks, "Odysseus, while he
loves his wife, endures seeing her weep over him" and adduces,
"His eyes were fixed as if they were horn or iron" (19.211) as his
illustrative citation. By contrast, "the suitors, who were in love
with the same woman, caught a glimpse of her," and "their limbs
went slack" (λύτο γούνατ') (18.212).

Pseudo-Plutarch's pair of Homeric passages is directly apposite to the situation Milton seeks to capture at this moment in

his poem. As the Son will later charge Adam, this is a moment in which he ought not "resign [his] manhood" (as iron Odysseus had not), but in which instead, immoderately, like the suitors, his knees slacken at the sight of Eve. (In his larger context, incidentally, Milton may also have in mind the line that follows in Homer's account of the suitors' reaction to Penelope, also cited in pseudo-Plutarch: "they all swore that they would lie beside her.") If Milton indeed had pseudo-Plutarch's commentary in mind when he composed his description of Adam's pusillanimous reaction to Eve's fatal trespass, then it is not enough simply to note the Homeric precedent for Milton's lines; we must also recall that the phrase λύτο γούνατα carried in Milton's day a particular semantic charge, lost in the intervening years (during which pseudo-Plutarch's commentary has dwindled from a viable interpretive treatise to a curiosity in the history of literary criticism).[59]

Whether and how one interprets an allusion is a function of one's historical moment. Allusions to earlier authors are not some diachronic phenomenon rendered obsolete by synchronic "cultural" study; they are no less "cultural" than any other textual phenomenon. The field of allusion studies desperately needs the insight—call it a new historical insight—that allusions are culturally mediated. Emerging out of a formalist or structuralist tradition, most recent treatments of allusion have attempted to liken verbal echo to other literary or rhetorical features such as metaphor or enthymeme and to treat the recognition and interpretation of an allusion as occurring almost automatically within the reading process. As I have shown, Ben-Porat speaks mechanistically of a "marker" and Garner of a "trigger," some feature of the alluding text that sends readers (automatically, it would seem) back to the source text. However, as common sense dictates (and our teaching of undergraduates regularly reveals), if the reader does not share a literary tradition with the alluding author, no form of marker will serve to evoke the source text. Formalist scholarship is, as Culler labels it, positivistic enough to find a scandal in a textual feature that only some readers will perceive, and that cannot conclusively be argued to be "there" in the poem. But a culturally oriented criticism finds no scandal here. Scholars who study allusions would do well to acknowledge how the recognition and interpretation of a verbal echo is culturally mediated and does not automatically occur in some transhistorically stable and predictable fashion.

The fact that allusion is culturally mediated also means, however, that the rejection of allusion by cultural studies has been unnecessary. Indeed, poststructuralism and new historicism only stand to benefit by readmitting the study of allusion. The opposition that Montrose implies when he contrasts "the diachronic text of an autonomous literary history" with "the synchronic text of a cultural system" is a false dichotomy. It is false in part because there is no such thing as a "diachronic text of an autonomous literary history." Milton alludes not to Homer, but to mid-seventeenth-century Homer, and Hume is attuned to late-seventeenth-century Homer, Newton to mid-eighteenth-century Homer, and so on. But Montrose's implied dichotomy is also false because "cultural systems" cannot be fully understood synchronically. Part of what cultures do is select from among the works that have been valued in the past, assign contemporary significance to those works, and pass them on to the next generation. (Indeed, one might argue that this diachronic activity better deserves the name *culture* than the hypostasized society-at-a-given-historical-moment that has been the focus of recent "cultural" analysis.)

Critics of new historicism, and new historicist critics themselves, have often remarked the irony that their commitment to synchronic study of historical "moments" means that they cannot easily construct histories in the most fundamental sense of that term: diachronic narratives of past events. New historicism is often praeterocentric without being, precisely, historical. The theory has not had a method for moving between one snapshot synchronic moment and the next. I propose that the sector of a culture that allows an author to allude and a reader to recognize and interpret that allusion, might provide a pivot point for

Montrose's axes of intertextuality, a point on which to move between synchronic and diachronic analyses of culture. To focus on that complex of agents and practices and of explicit standards and implicit assumptions by which a particular society assigns value and meaning to cultural artifacts—the complex within which allusions find their conditions of possibility and significance—might helpfully provide cultural studies with the means to discuss the process of enculturation and new historicism the means to write histories.

The phenomenon of allusion, especially the species of allusion that I have here referred to as phraseological adaptation, is a literary device involving subtle artistry and playful erudition; the impact of allusions on the meaning of a literary work can be significant and far-reaching. The study of allusion, however, has been hampered by limiting assumptions and an imprecise technical vocabulary, as well as by the claims made on behalf of other forms of intertextuality, which have consigned such study to a position of little prestige within the field of literary criticism at large. Allusion is a more artful and resonant literary device than our critical vocabulary has allowed us to appreciate. Moreover, it lies at the nexus of some important strains of contemporary literary criticism and theory. I would argue that the phenomenon deserves greater critical and theoretical attention than it has drawn. The ensuing chapters seek in some measure to redress the relative critical neglect of the device, and to model what a historically and culturally oriented approach to the phenomenon might look like.

Two

"Dire Example"

The War in Heaven
as Admonitory Exemplum

The most explicitly Homeric portion of *Paradise Lost* is surely the war in heaven, narrated in books 5 and 6 of Milton's epic. It is no surprise, then, that allusions to Homer's epics, especially the *Iliad*, are frequent within these books and that the episode can therefore illustrate in a particularly comprehensive way Milton's techniques of alluding to Homer. In the course of this chapter, I will scrutinize many Homeric passages reprised by Milton and suggest what they lend to the meaning of the episode. But I will also try to establish that the Homeric epics exerted a different kind of influence on the war in heaven episode, beyond what they contribute to enriching the meaning of particular passages. The largest argument of this book is that, in his own efforts to write something that aftertimes should not willingly let die, Milton reflected on the grounds of Maeonides's "renown," or, as we might put it today, in his own efforts to write a canonical work of literature, Milton attempted to exploit the same cultural mechanisms by which Homer's epics were being canonically reproduced in his own day. The war in heaven episode provides a focused portion of the epic in which to study one of the mechanisms of canonization operative in the early modern period: namely, the expectation that major poems should include moral exempla.

I will begin that study with a reexamination of the tradition of critical commentary on the war in heaven, an episode that has proved troublesome for critics of Milton. Early critics debated the artistic quality of the episode, and this represented the core issue raised by the narrative until Arnold Stein attempted to resolve that debate by addressing what he regarded as a more fundamental issue: the issue of genre. However, his generic reclassification of the episode as a mock-epic has itself proven to be controversial. This chapter considers these issues of assessment and classification by examining comprehensively the nature of Milton's appropriation of Homer in the episode. The one previous examination of Milton's allusions to Homer, that of George de Forest Lord, bolsters Stein's classification of the episode as a mock-epic but does so by isolating for discussion only a certain strain of Homeric allusions within the episode. A more complete examination of Milton's allusions to Homer will compel us to modify Lord's conclusions, which in turn will suggest a different classification of the episode, as well as a different understanding of the critical response that the episode has provoked.

In the course of this account, I will consider the term by which early modern writers characterized their relation to their precursors. Writers of Milton's era did not primarily regard their precursors as having created "sources" or "subtexts" to which they could allude in order to reinforce or qualify the meaning of passages in their own poems. Instead, they spoke of Homer and Virgil as providing models or examples of how to construct a poem; moreover, what the classical poets' practice revealed is that a poem should be built out of exempla: stories that depict behavior that should be imitated or avoided. With this in mind, I propose that book 6 is most fruitfully classified rhetorically, rather than generically — as an extended negative exemplum.[1]

This reclassification will allow a fuller understanding of the function of allusions within the episode, and thereby a fuller understanding of allusion generally speaking. Allusions, I will show, generally have an intrinsically evaluative dimension, lauding or correcting their source text. A reprise pays a certain kind of homage to the source to which it gestures, but also lodges a certain kind of criticism, if only the faint, implicit criticism that the original author did not exhaust the signifying possibilities of the spur. This double-edged quality of echoes serves in book 6 of *Paradise Lost* to underscore an ambiguity that is intrinsic to negative exempla. The tensions inherent in this rhetorical device are similar to the inherent ambiguity of allusions. A negative exemplum must negotiate contradictory demands. It must present a particular figure's actions as serious and then dismiss them; it must respect, without seeming to honor. In the particular case of Raphael's narration, Satan must be made to appear to be an epic threat, yet be treated with mock-epic scorn. Allusions, which are marked by a similar evaluative tension, serve to stimulate the faculty of judgment; in this central episode of *Paradise Lost* they elicit the critical response the epic demands of, and exercises in, its audience.

Incongruities in the War in Heaven

The war in heaven, narrated in books 5 and 6 of *Paradise Lost*, has long been a troublesome episode for critics of Milton. Early commentators debated the quality of the episode. Addison, for instance, generally admired Milton's account of the war, though he took exception to Satan's punning; by contrast, Samuel Johnson thought the episode flawed by "incongruity" that was especially evident in "the confusion of spirit and matter."[2] In the 1950s Arnold Stein attempted to resolve the critical debates the episode

had engendered by addressing what he proposed as a more fundamental issue: that of the episode's genre. By regarding book 6 as
a mock-epic, a "great scherzo" ridiculing Satan's attempt to gain
spiritual superiority through the material means of armed conflict, Stein sought to reconcile Johnson's reservations with earlier
readers' esteem for the episode, arguing that the same "confusion
of spirit and matter" that makes the narrative an artistic failure
as an epic makes it a success as mock-epic.[3]

Despite Stein's attempt to resolve the critical debate, however,
the war in heaven episode has remained troublesome—only now
it is the genre of the episode that seems difficult to determine.
David Farley-Hills speaks for many when he claims that he cannot share Stein's view of the episode as uniformly burlesque:
"Unfortunately Milton does not exploit the comic material and
tries to pretend that the battle is genuinely heroic. The mock-
heroic element is thus obscured and the solemn tone runs counter to the logic of the action."[4] This tonal inconsistency, this mix
of serious and mocking elements in the episode, has prompted a
variety of generic classifications, but has prevented scholarly con-
sensus regarding the genre of the episode. Isabel MacCaffrey suggests that the episode can be *either* epic or mock-epic, "depending
on whether we read as man or as God." Barbara Lewalski claims
that "the tone remains substantially heroic until the invention
of the canon....Milton shifts the generic frame to mock epic at
just this moment to signal a decline from the flawed heroism of
Homeric battle to the thoroughly ignoble warfare fought with
'demonic' modern weapons." David Quint speaks of the *Iliad* as
a "major epic model behind the war in Milton's heaven," but,
without making the nature of the connection clear, claims that
Milton also "openly mocks the individual martial heroics" of the
Iliad.[5] The generic indeterminacy of the narrative has prompted
at least one Miltonist to return to the critical approach characteristic of the episode's early critics. For James Wooten the episode is an aesthetic failure: it is "woven of so many incompatible
strands" because "what had been projected to be a Homeric nar-

rative...was rewritten to reflect the bitter disappointment of the Restoration" and this rewriting "is not totally successful."[6]

In this chapter I will focus on a third issue, one that almost all of the critics who have considered the episode implicitly agree underlies the critical and generic questions, but which has only once been formulated explicitly. One might call this question an intertextual one, in the broad sense of the term *intertextual:* I will be asking what sort of relationship books 5 and 6 of *Paradise Lost* adopt toward their primary source text or subtext, the *Iliad.* This question is closely related to the generic question, for if the episode is intended as a mock-epic, it would presumably adopt a dismissive stance toward the ethos manifested in the Homeric poems, whereas if it is intended to be read as serious epic, it would presumably take up an emulative stance toward Homer. But the intertextual question is independent of, and indeed more fundamental than, the generic question in a way that may be briefly illustrated by observing the clarity that intertextual analysis lends to generic classifications.

When critics call books 5 and 6 of *Paradise Lost* a mock-epic, they mean to say that the war in heaven ridicules traditional epic values of martial prowess and heroism; it mocks epic. But the term *mock-epic* more usually applies to compositions that admiringly invoke traditional epic values in order to mock contemporary pettiness—as, for instance, Alexander Pope's *Rape of the Lock* invokes traditional epic to mock the pettiness of eighteenth century polite society.[7] The meaning of the generic label, then, is largely dependent on the attitude that the later work exhibits toward the former, that is, on the nature of the intertextual relationship.

I undertake a more detailed and complete examination than has hitherto been offered of Milton's relation to Homer in this episode. Such an intertextual study—attending closely to Milton's allusive practice as well as to the intertextual theories of the early modern period—will allow a more accurate and fruitful classification of the episode narrated in books 5 and 6—but a rhetorical, rather than a generic, classification. The episode, I will argue, is best understood as a negative or admonitory exemplum. This reclassification in turn provides a fresh way of considering the critical debate the episode has prompted. As an exemplum, the episode necessarily includes both epic and mock-epic strains, and by considering this range of attitudes that Milton expresses toward the martial values celebrated by Homer, we may come to understand the critical debate that the episode has provoked as a function of the sustained evaluative response its allusions demand of its readers.

The Range of Milton's Homeric Appropriations

The nature of Milton's appropriation in books 5 and 6 of material from Homer and other epic precursors has rarely been the object of direct critical scrutiny.[8] Indeed, Addison and Johnson's disagreement over the *quality* of books 5 and 6 is grounded on their shared assumption concerning the *kind* of appropriation the episode involves. Both critics think Milton is trying to reproduce a miniature *Iliad* in the center of his own epic; Addison thinks he succeeds, Johnson thinks he fails. And even though Stein challenges their assumption as to the kind of appropriation this episode involves, he spends no more time than they do on direct examination of Milton's allusions. The one critic who has foregrounded Milton's appropriation of Homer is George de Forest Lord. He maintains that Milton "[drew] on theomachies in the *Iliad* to shape some of the key incidents in the war in Heaven and, above all, to set the tone for the central episodes in it." Lord's argument is intended to support Stein's claim that the episode is a "great scherzo" by arguing, "when gods fight each other or fight with mortals, they may suffer pain, but immortality invariably renders the divine victim ludicrous."[9] Lord finds a cunning artistry in Milton's use of Homeric material; he argues that Milton appropriates one strain in the *Iliad* (the mock-epic strain latent in Homer's theomachies) in order to ridicule another, more dominant strain in the *Iliad:* the ideal of martial valor celebrated in the epic.[10]

Lord's argument, though, oversimplifies the allusive practice evident in books 5 and 6 of *Paradise Lost.* Allusions to Homer's theomachies hardly predominate in this episode, nor are references to Homer's divinities invariably concerned with the gods' ludicrous immortality.

By what principle of selection he isolates allusions to Homer's theomachies as the dominant type of allusion in this episode, Lord never makes clear. In fact, allusions that liken the loyal and rebel angels to prominent human warriors in the *Iliad* far outnumber those that liken them to Homer's gods. For instance, Satan's flyting with Michael—"nor think thou with wind / Of airie threats to aw whom yet with deeds / Thou canst not" (*PL* 6.282–84)—allusively associates him with Aeneas, who similarly dismisses Achilles's threats: "Son of Peleus, never hope by words to frighten me" (*Iliad* 20.200). In like manner, when the loyal angels are described as "[moving] on / *In silence* thir bright Legions, to the sound / Of instrumental Harmonie that *breath'd / Heroic Ardor* to advent'rous deeds" (*PL* 6.63–66; emphasis added), they resemble humans: the Greek troops, who, Homer says, "went silently, breathing valor" (*Iliad* 3.8).

Moving beyond the level of brief phraseological adaptation, we find that Milton's imitations of whole Homeric scenes also link the angelic warriors with Homer's mortals as often as with his immortals. For example, the initial confrontation between the hosts of rebel and loyal angels is closely modeled on the first confrontation between the Achaeans and Trojans narrated in book 3 of the *Iliad.* Such details as the "cloudy Van" of troops (*PL* 6.107; *Iliad* 3.10) and Satan's "vast and haughtie strides" (*PL* 6.109; *Iliad* 3.22) were seemingly gleaned from Homer's description. Moreover, the structure of Milton's scene is modeled on that of Homer. In both passages the armies near each other, then stop to allow a pair of champions to emerge for a monomachia. In both epics, this initial contest highlights the reason behind the larger conflict of which it is a part: in the *Iliad*, Helen's legitimate and illegitimate husbands contend; in *Paradise Lost*, it is the faithful and the rebellious angel. In both cases the underlying issue is one of fidelity and, although each duel is inconclusive, the party in the right gets the better of the exchange, presaging the ultimate downfall of the offending party and his allies. In any event, the angels are likened not to Homer's ludicrously immortal gods, but to the mortals Paris and Menelaus.

Not only does Lord ignore allusions that liken Milton's angelic characters to Homer's mortals, but he also ignores those that emphasize other features of the angelic soldiers than their ludicrous immortality. For example, when Satan commences his rebellion by awakening Beelzebub, his words, "Sleep'st thou?" virtually translate the εὕδεις with which the evil dream sent by Zeus awakens Agamemnon in book 2 of the *Iliad* (*PL* 5.673; *Iliad* 2.23). It is certainly not so much Satan's immortality as his deceitfulness that Milton intends to stress through this allusion. Similarly, when Satan sends Abdiel off with a threat that recalls Agamemnon's threat to the priest Chryses, it is again clearly not Satan's immortality that is being emphasized but his tyrannical nature (*PL* 5.868; *Iliad* 1.32).

Even within the scene that Lord most closely examines, his exclusive focus on allusions to Homer's theomachia leads him to neglect an allusion that does something other than underscore Satan's absurdity. He remarks that Michael's wounding of Satan combines elements from two divine woundings in the *Iliad*, book 5: while it is primarily modeled on Diomedes's wounding of Ares, the phrase "a stream of Nectarous humor...such as Celestial Spirits may bleed" echoes Homer's description of Aphrodite's wound (*PL* 6.332; *Iliad* 5.339–40). But Lord fails to note that the description that follows, the description of Satan's rescue by the rebel host, is modeled on the Trojans' rescue of Hector in book 14 of the *Iliad*:

Forthwith on all sides to his aide was run
By Angels many and strong, who interpos'd
Defense, while others bore him on their Shields
Back to his Chariot, where it stood retir'd
From off the files of war.   (*PL* 6.335–39)

        no man was heedless of [Hector], but rather
sloped the strong circles of their shields over him, while his
   companions
caught him in their arms out of the fighting and reached his
   fast-footed
horses, where they stood to the rear of the fighting and the battle
holding their charioteer and the elaborate chariot,
and these carried him, groaning heavily, back toward the city.
                                    (*Iliad* 14.427–32)

If the resemblance to Ares emphasizes that Satan is ultimately invulnerable, and therefore absurd as a combatant, the reference to Hector must do something else. Perhaps it suggests that, though the physical aspect of Satan's wound will be short lived, that wound nevertheless does represent a permanent injury in the form of a loss of status. The allusion may, moreover, add a note of plangency to the absurdity for which Lord argues; for though Satan is like Hector in being a degree less glorious than he was a moment before, he is still unlike Hector in that he cannot die a meaningful, heroic death. Not just ludicrous, Satan is pathetic.

Lord's thesis that allusions to Homer in books 5 and 6 of *Paradise Lost* serve principally to make Satan appear absurd, besides neglecting allusions that show him as deceitful, tyrannical, and pathetic, also overlooks allusions that are not meant to undercut, deflate, or ironize. For example, when Abdiel, in resisting Satan's rebellion, is described as "fearless, though alone / Encompass'd round with foes," the language resembles that which Agamemnon uses to describe Tydeus, Diomedes's father: "There, stranger though he was...Tydeus, was not frightened, alone among so many Kadmeians" (*PL* 5.875–78; *Iliad* 4.387–88). Surely we are not to think, "Abdiel seems courageous here, but

I know that in fact he cannot be physically harmed, so his courage is inconsequential and absurd." Surely we are to admire his bravery even as Agamemnon admires that of Tydeus. Or again, the celestial warriors are once described as "fierce encount'ring Angels," assaulting each other so violently that "all Heav'n / Resounded, and had Earth bin then, all Earth / Had to her Center shook," a description inspired by the theomachia in the *Iliad*, book 20, in which "the gods came driving together in wrath," so violently that Hades "sprang from his throne and screamed aloud, for fear that above him / he who circles the land, Poseidon, might break the earth open" (*PL* 6.217–20; *Iliad* 20.54–66). Is this allusion meant to convey the inconsequential nature of divine warfare or, quite the contrary, its terrifying potency? And even if Milton is content to make the faithful angels absurd, can we really imagine him undercutting even the Father and the Son in that way? Yet Milton's God is several times allusively linked to Zeus; the Son once to Zeus and several times to Apollo.[11] Milton's relation to Homer, then, is far more complex than Lord's thesis would suggest.

Exempla

If Lord is unable to account for the variety of uses to which Homeric material is put in the war in heaven episode, it is perhaps because the very term that guides his examination of Milton's relation to Homer, *allusion*, figures the nature of intertextual relationships very differently than early modern authors themselves imagined it. The conventional understanding of the term *allusion*, as I established in the preceding chapter, is that it names a poetic phenomenon in which a brief verbal recollection of a phrase from an earlier text establishes a relationship with that earlier text that enriches or qualifies the significance of the passage in which the reprise appears. Most contemporary critics understand allusion as a local poetic effect and a phenomenon properly eliciting a hermeneutic response. Early modern writers, by contrast, wrote of prior authors less as providing them with the means for enriching the significance of their works and more as providing them with models for composition. The relations they established with classical authors figured more in the making than the meaning of their works and were thus more a matter of poetics than of hermeneutics.

The term they used to name the relationship between the work of a later poet and that of his precursors was not *allusion* but *example*. In his letter to Raleigh, Edmund Spenser describes the technique of "all the antique Poets historicall"—Homer, Virgil, Ariosto, and Tasso—by "ensample of which excellente Poets, [he] labour[ed] to pourtraict in Arthure, before he was king, the image of a brave knight, perfected in the twelue priuate morall vertues."[12] Milton similarly regarded Aeschylus, Sophocles, and Euripides "the best rule to all who endeavor to write Tragedy" and therefore, "according to antient rule, and best example" circumscribed the action of *Samson Agonistes* within the space of 24 hours (CM 1:333). He thought in these terms, moreover, about the possible influence of his own work: the measure of *Paradise Lost*—"heroic verse without rime, as that of Homer in Greek and of Virgil in Latin"—would recover an exemplary dimension of classical epic and therefore allow *Paradise Lost* itself to stand to later authors as "an example set, the first in English, of ancient liberty recovered to Heroic Poem from the troublesome and modern bondage of Riming" (CM 2:6).

What did early modern writers learn about poetic composition when they turned to the ancient poets as examples? Aside from learning technical matters such as meter and the dramatic unities, they saw poetry that was exemplary in another sense of the word: poetry that included characters who exemplify various virtues and vices. In his *Discourses on the Heroic Poem*, Torquato Tasso describes the purpose of poetry as "to help men by the example of human deeds."[13] Sir Philip Sidney asserts that the "faining [of] notable images of vertues vices, or what els" is "the right describing note to know a Poet by." The peerless poet surpasses the historian and the philosopher, "for whatsoever the philosopher saith should be done, he gives a perfect picture of it by some one, by whom he presupposeth it was done; so as he coupleth the generall notion with the particuler example."[14] Spenser thought that by "colour[ing his work] with an historicall fiction" he could entice readers to the "profite of ensample."[15] And Milton hoped his great poetic work would prove "doctrinal and exemplary to a nation" and imagined himself "teaching over the whole book of sanctity and virtu through all the instances of example" (CM 3:239).

Thus, in the early modern period classical poets like Homer were exemplary in two senses: they included in their poetry patterns of virtue and vice, and they taught later authors to do the same. Spenser's letter to Raleigh succinctly captures these two senses of poetic exemplarity. He writes that he has

> followed all the antique Poets historicall, first Homere, who in the Persons of Agamemnon and Ulysses hath *ensampled* a good governour and a vertuous man, the one in his Ilias, the other in his Odysseis: then Virgil, whose like intention was to do in the person of Aeneas: after him Ariosto comprised them both in his Orlando: and lately Tasso disseevered them againe, and formed both parts in two persons, namely that part which they in Philosophy call Ethice, or vertues of a private man, coloured in his Rinaldo: The other named Politice in his Godfredo. By *ensample* of which excellente Poets, I labour to pourtraict in Arthure, before he was king, the image of a brave knight, perfected in the twelve private morall vertues.[16]

Spenser has followed his predecessors' poetic example by creating an exemplary character.

To recall the terms in which early modern writers conceived of the relations between their texts and those of their precursors points the way to a reclassification of the war in heaven episode. The reason that generic classification has proven so difficult for recent criticism is that the episode should be classified rhetorically rather than generically. The episode is best understood as an exemplum. It is, after all, twice labeled as such: once by the internal narrator who renders the account and again by the over-all narrator of the epic. Raphael concludes his narration by warn-ing Adam, "let it profit thee to have heard / By terrible Example the reward / Of disobedience" (6.909–11). And, after the intro-duction to book 7, the narrator resumes his account of the con-ference between Adam and Raphael by asking his muse to "Say Goddess, what ensu'd when Raphael, / The affable Arch-angel, had forewarn'd / Adam by dire example to beware / Apostasy" (7.40–43).

Consider the episode in the light of J. A. Mosher's definition of the device. He summarizes the purposes served by exempla as follows: "(1) to furnish a concrete illustration of the result of obeying or disobeying some religious or moral law; (2) to give proof or confirmation of the truth of an assertion; (3) to arouse fear in the sinful or to stimulate the zeal of the godly; (4) to make clear the meaning of some abstruse statement; (5) to revive lan-guid listeners, evoke interest or laughter; (6) to eke out a scant sermon by 'farsing' it with tales."[17]

Most of these attributes are clearly evident in Raphael's tale. The episode is explicitly designed to "(1) furnish a concrete illus-tration of the result of obeying or disobeying some religious or moral law." The story is begun when Adam asks about Raphael's phrase "If ye be found obedient" and, as we have seen, Raphael concludes the episode by calling it a "terrible example [of] the reward / Of disobedience." (PL 5.501, 513–14; 6.910–11). The epi-sode also serves to "(2) give proof or confirmation of the truth of an assertion." Adam incredulously asks,

> can we want obedience then
> To him, or possibly his love desert
> Who form'd us from the dust, and plac'd us here
> Full to the utmost measure of what bliss
> Human desires can seek or apprehend?   (5.514–18)

Raphael's tale elaborates on his claim that, yes, "some are fall'n, to disobedience fall'n" (5.541). The story is designed "(3) to arouse fear...[and] stimulate zeal" and "(5) to relieve languid listeners."

God sends Raphael to Adam to "warne him to beware / He swerve not too secure" and Raphael's final words to Adam are "remember, and fear to transgress" (5.238–39, 6.912). Within the admonitory exemplum of Satan's disobedience, the story of Abdiel "then whom none with more zeale ador'd / The Deitie" (6.805–06), serves as an interpolated positive exemplum designed to model godly zeal and obedience.[18] Finally, the episode serves "(4) to make clear the meaning of some abstruse statement": Raphael's initially puzzling "If ye be found obedient."

To classify the war in heaven rhetorically, as an exemplum, can enhance our appreciation of the episode in several ways. For one, it casts a new light on Raphael's famously cryptic introductory comment. "What surmounts the reach / Of human sense," he tells Adam, "I shall delineate so, / By lik'ning spiritual to corporal forms, / As may express them best"; then he qualifies this statement by asking, "though what if Earth / Be but the shaddow of Heav'n, and things therein / Each to other like, more then on earth is thought?" (5.571–76). Raphael's interrogative suggestion has implications for our understanding of the episode that follows—and indeed for understanding Milton's mimetic theory generally. But statements like Raphael's are also a convention of exempla; such claims are instances of what might be referred to as the "this is no fable" topos.[19] In order to be persuasive, an exemplum must be regarded as actually having occurred, and instances of the device often include explicit claims of veracity like that of Raphael.

For a second way in which our appreciation of the war in heaven episode is enhanced by regarding it as an exemplum, I turn to one of the characteristics of exemplum enumerated by Jeffrey Lyons in his treatment of the device: namely, iterativity. For an example to be persuasive, the audience must perceive it as being something that has happened or can happen repeatedly: "It is impossible to consider as an example the manifestation of a class of one."[20] For this reason, speakers will frequently present their audience with two or more examples (or imply that the one example they do provide is a member of a larger set of similar examples). When books 5 and 6 of *Paradise Lost* are considered in this light, the suspense surrounding Adam and Eve's potential disobedience is considerably heightened. For the story of Satan's rebellion in fact *is* a manifestation of a class of one; when Raphael cites it, it is the only instance of a creature's disobedience to God. It is *iterable,* but has not yet been *iterated.* Whether or not Satan's story will prove to be an example, in fact, rests in Adam and Eve's hands. And the way the episode therefore trembles on the verge of its stated classification nicely heightens our sense of Adam and Eve's genuine freedom, while subtly forecasting their fall.

The most important benefit of viewing books 5 and 6 as an exemplum, however, is that such a perspective helps to explain the coexistence of epic and mock-epic strains that have proven so troublesome to critics who consider the episode. Since Stein, critics have argued that the war in heaven is one or the other, epic or mock-epic—without ever suggesting that it might, coherently and simultaneously, be both. The inherent tensions of the rhetorical device are such, however, that the war in heaven, as an exemplum, *must* contain both epic and mock-epic elements. An admonitory or negative exemplum (as most are), presenting a figure whose behavior is to be avoided, must negotiate contradictory demands.[21] It must condemn that figure's actions, and yet treat them as serious. Without seeming to honor, it must nevertheless pay a degree of respect. In the particular case of Raphael's narration, Satan must be made to appear an epic threat, yet be treated with mocking scorn. The presence of both epic and mock-epic strains in the episode, which has proved so troublesome to critics, is best explained, then, by regarding the episode as a particular subspecies—namely, the admonitory or negative exemplum—of the broad rhetorical category under which I have suggested it be classified.

"Involv'd and Interwoven"

What this mix of sincere and mocking strains means for our understanding of the episode's intertextuality is that we must not expect the relation between Milton and Homer manifested within the imitation to be simple and uniform. We must not expect (with Addison and Johnson) that Milton's response to his great precursor in heroic poetry will be simply one of admiring imitation, nor (with Stein and Lord) that it will invariably be one of mocking dismissal.

Milton adopts a variety of stances toward Homer. In expanding Lord's limited picture of the uses to which Milton puts Homeric material, I have already in some measure suggested the range of Milton's appropriational strategies. But a more direct analysis of Milton's appropriations—imitative, emulative, and critical—will allow me to expand upon the qualities of allusion studied in the previous chapter, at the same time that it enables a new approach to the long-standing debate as to the quality of the war in heaven episode.[22]

Some of Milton's allusions are closely imitative. Raphael's description of the conflicting armies' courage—"no thought of flight / None of retreat, no unbecoming deed / That argu'd fear"—seems to be modeled on Hecuba's description of Hector: "with no thought in his mind of flight or withdrawal" (*PL* 6.236–38; *Iliad* 24.226). The "hostile frown / And visage all inflam'd" of Michael recalls a description of Agamemnon, whose "two eyes showed like fire in their blazing" (*PL* 6.260; *Iliad* 1.104). When Zophiel exhorts the loyal angels, "let each / His Adamantine coat gird well, and each / Fit well his helme, grip fast his orbed Shield," his speech is modeled on Agamemnon's command to the Greek troops to prepare for battle:

> εὖ μέν τις δόρυ θηξάσθω, εὖ δ᾽ ἀσπίδα θέσθω,
> εὖ δέ τις ἵπποισιν δεῖπνον δότω ὠκυπόδεσσιν
> εὖ δέ τις ἅρματος ἀμφὶς ἰδὼν πολέμοιο μεδέσθω
>
> [Well let each man sharpen his spear and well compose his shield,
> Well too let each man feed his swift-footed horses,
> Well too let each man look over his chariot.]
>
> (*PL* 6.541–43; *Iliad* 2.382–84)

In his reprise, Milton seems to want to capture the effect of Homer's anaphora of εὖ...τις through his own epistrophe of "each" and midline repetition of "well." When Milton wants to stress the genuine heroism of the loyal angels, then, he employs fairly straightforward adaptations of Homeric lines and passages.

A second relationship Milton adopts toward Homer is that of rival. This stance too involves implicitly paying tribute to his precursor; but it also implies a criticism that Homer did not go far enough. For instance, Milton describes the escalation of the war in heaven as follows:

> and now all Heav'n
> Had gon to wrack, with ruin overspred,
> Had not th' Almightie Father where he sits
> Shrin'd in his Sanctuarie of Heav'n secure,
> Consulting on the sum of things, forseen
> This tumult, and permitted all, advis'd.   (6.669–74)

This is an allusion to a moment in the eighth book of the *Iliad:* "And now there would have been fighting beyond control, and destruction, / now they would have been driven and penned like sheep against Ilion, / had not the father of gods and men sharply perceived them" (130–32). The "and now...had not" structure is imitated, but beside Milton's reprise, "all Heav'n [going] to wrack," Homer's spur, the Trojans being "penned like sheep," looks laughably insignificant. Some forms of rivalry are almost mechanical, as when Milton gives Satan a shield "of tenfold Adamant," where the shield made by Hephaistos for Achilles had only five folds (*PL* 6.254–55; *Iliad* 18.481). Others are more subtle, as when Milton expands on the personification implicit in Homer's "rosy-fingered Dawn": "Morn, / Wak't by the circling Hours, with rosie hand, / Unbarr'd the gates of Light" (6.2–4).

A form of rivalry slightly more critical than these instances of epic topping is that whereby Milton explicitly or implicitly corrects Homer by suggesting that, while he is the later poet, the events narrated in *Paradise Lost* are earlier—and more accurately depicted—than those narrated in the *Iliad.* Harold Bloom, as we shall see more fully in chapter 4, has made much of such passages.[23] The most famous example of this strategy is in book 1, where Milton recounts Homer's story of Mulciber, then corrects it: "thus they relate, / Erring; for he with this rebellious rout / Fell long before" (1.746–48). But there is an instance in book 6 as well. Raphael describes to Adam the approach of the angels:

> high above the ground
> Thir march was, and the passive Air upbore
> Thir nimble tread; as when the total kind
> Of Birds in orderly array on wing
> Came summond over Eden to receive
> Thir names of thee.   (71–76)

This comparison of warriors to birds recalls a passage in the second book of the *Iliad* that describes the Greek troops:

> These, as the multitudinous nations of birds winged,
> of geese, and of cranes, and of swans long-throated
> in the Asian meadow beside the Kastrian waters
> this way and that way make their flights in the pride of their
>   wings, then
> settle in clashing swarms and the whole meadow echoes with
>   them,
> so of these the multitudinous tribes from the ships and
> shelters poured to the plain of Skamandros.   (459–65)

The significant difference is that Milton has replaced the bird names — geese, cranes, and swans — with a reference to the fact that Adam gave names to the birds, thus subtly stressing the priority, and implicitly the accuracy, of events as narrated in *Paradise Lost*.

Finally, Milton can be directly critical of his precursor. In the proem to book 9, he is overtly critical, reducing the subject of classical epics to wrath, rage, and ire:

> the wrath
> Of Stern *Achilles* on his Foe pursued
> Thrice Fugitive about Troy Wall; or rage
> Of *Turnus* for *Lavinia* disespous'd,
> Or *Neptune's* ire or *Juno's*, that so long
> Perplex'd the Greek and *Cytherea's* son.   (14–19)

He similarly reduces the narrative of such epics to the "long and tedious havoc" of "battles feigned" (30–31). But his criticism can be implicit as well, as when he portrays Moloch threatening "at his Chariot wheels to drag [Gabriel] bound"; Homer's Achilles, who is famous for dragging his enemy behind his chariot, is through this allusion implicitly presented as diabolical (6.359).[24]

No monochromatic picture of Milton's relation to Homer will suffice. The martial heroism of earlier epics is neither wholly admirable nor entirely corrupt. We are compelled in the case of each allusion to determine what evaluation Milton is making of his poetic precursors and the values their poems celebrate. The variety in Milton's allusions invites the kind of critical engagement that Milton envisions in *Aeropagitica* as appropriate to moral decision making: "the knowledge of good is so involv'd and interwoven with the knowledge of evil, and in so many cunning resemblances hardly to be discern'd, that those confused seeds which were impos'd on Psyche as an incessant labor to cull out and sort asunder, were not more intermixt" (CM 4:310). For Milton, virtue demands careful scrutiny of minute particulars and the constant readiness to evaluate and reevaluate—precisely the exercise his allusions offer the reader. If we return, then, to the critical debate that books 5 and 6 of *Paradise Lost* have prompted, we realize that that debate is not merely an accident of historically varying tastes but a natural consequence of the episode's internal dynamics, a result of the sustained evaluative engagement that the episode and its Homeric allusions demand of its readers.

THREE

"A Fabric Wonderful"

The Marvelous and Verisimilar
in Milton's Christian Epic

In the previous chapter, I studied Milton's relation to Homer by considering a single episode within *Paradise Lost:* the war in heaven. I now move to a dimension of this interpoetic relationship that manifests itself throughout the entirety of Milton's epic. The discursive mechanism of canonization on which I focus is the phrase "Christian epic." As Thomas Greene says, "from Petrarch's youth to Milton's age Europe awaited the poet and the poem which would demonstrate the equality of the modern age to antiquity."[1] And, he argues, this expectation expressed itself in the notion of a Christian epic, an ideal whose successful realization would secure an author immense prestige. The ideal of the Christian epic functioned as a pre-established canonical slot (something like "the great American novel," perhaps), to be occupied by whoever might persuasively fulfill the expectations implicit within the ideal.

But *Christian epic* is not so much a category enabling literary production as it is problem to be solved. For as Milton quite clearly saw, "the better fortitude of Patience and Heroic Martyrdom" does not lend itself to narration within a genre that has hitherto deemed "Warrs...the onely Argument / Heroic" (*PL* 9.28–31). I argue that Milton solves this so-called "problem of Christian epic" by radically reconceiving the fundamental characteristics of the genre of epic. Rather than follow Virgil in defining the genre in terms of a set of martial episodes, Milton locates the essence of the epic in a particular aesthetic effect suggested to him by Homer's formulaic diction, and captured by him in his own allusive style in which the phrases are simultaneously elevated and yet familiar. Even where no hermeneutic connection is established by the allusive phraseology, something as simple as the mere familiarity of verbal echoes can be aesthetically and canonically functional.

The Problem of Christian Epic

Like a host of other Renaissance writers, Milton confronted what has been termed (in the subtitle of Judith Kates's book on him and Tasso) "the problem of Christian epic."[2] From the time the concept first appeared in Italian literary criticism (in Lorenzo Gambara's 1576 *Tractatio de perfectae poeseos ratione*), an incompatibility has been seen in the terms *Christian* and *epic*.[3] The problem, as it is usually formulated, stems from the difference between the value system to which Christians adhere and the one celebrated in pagan epic; a ubiquitous word in criticism that takes up the topic of Christian epic is "revaluation." The Renaissance writer wanted to depict characters and events admirable from a Christian point of view—"the better fortitude / Of Patience and Heroic Martyrdom" (*PL* 9.31–32)—but the genre in which he wanted to compose, the exalted genre of epic, was characterized by a conventional set of episodes pertaining to "Warrs, hitherto the onely Argument / Heroic deem'd" (*PL* 9.28–29), episodes for the most part incompatible with a Christian theme. In Thomas Greene's formulation of the problem of Christian epic, "really to count, the new work would have to look like the *Aeneid*," by which he means that the events narrated in a would-be Christian epic would have to be the ones with which readers of classical epic are familiar.[4] Yet little of what is important to Christianity looks like the events narrated in the *Aeneid*.

Nevertheless, critics argue, Milton did manage to "solve" the problem of Christian epic, and his doing so accounts in some measure for the canonical status of his poem. The standard argument runs as follows. Milton associates traditional epic material with characters condemned in his poems: with Satan and his cohorts, or with such figures as Sin and Death. The inclusion of such material makes the poem epic; its condemnation makes the poem Christian. John Steadman is the primary exponent of this view. According to Steadman, by "invest[ing] Satan with traditional heroic attributes," Milton "exposes the heroic pretences of these traditional heroes [Achilles and Odysseus] as essentially diabolical.... Milton's 'heroic' archfiend turns out to be an ingenious literary device for reassessing the heroic tradition. The paradox of a 'godlike' devil enables him to arraign epic and history alike for mistaking brutishness for heroic virtue, and thus celebrating the counterfeit idol of heroism."[5]

The strategy Steadman here describes Milton may have derived from Tasso. Kates, picking up on Steadman's hint that "this technique was not altogether original," demonstrates how Tasso anticipates Milton's method. She claims that in *Jerusalem Delivered* "classical allusions, images derived from Graeco-Roman mythology and overt uses of ancient literature or history are almost exclusively confined to situations that involve pagan characters or demons," especially Solyman and Argantes.[6] One problem with the arguments Steadman and Kates advance is that they neglect the significant number of classical allusions that pertain to characters admired by Milton and Tasso: Godfrey, Adam and Eve, and even God. Francis Blessington shows, contra Steadman, how allusions to classical epic underlie all aspects of *Paradise Lost*.[7] And, if one is willing to consider not only overt references, but also "covert allusions" (that is, verbal echoes of pagan epic), it would not be difficult to demonstrate that this is true of *Jerusalem Delivered* as well.

But the real weakness of the argument that Milton solved the "problem of Christian epic" by associating elements of classical epic with Satan is that this is not, in the end, much of a solution; for if recognizably epic material is relegated to only a portion of a poem, and a devalued portion at that, in what sense is that poem an epic? Presumably, one aspect of the problem of Christian epic is the necessity of making one's poem recognizably epic *in its entirety*. The solution offered by critics such as Steadman and Kates ignores this necessity. To accept it as our account of the way these two poets confronted the problem of Christian epic is to miss how radically Milton—following leads provided to him in the theory and practice of Tasso—reconceived the fundamental characteristics of the genre of epic.

Episodic Imitation

The problem of Christian epic is, in a word, Virgil. As Martin Mueller observes, "Virgil provided later epic poets not only with a model to imitate; his use of Homer also established a *method* of imitation." Virgil's method is to imitate at the level of the episode. Mueller states, "Virgil counterpointed his revaluation of Homeric values with a scrupulous imitation of the formal conventions and *plot patterns* of the Homeric epics. The *Aeneid* aims at including all the significant *actions* of both *Iliad* and *Odyssey* within the confines of one epic."[8] By itself, the revaluation involved in replacing pagan ideals with Christian ones is not "the problem of Christian epic." Indeed, Virgil's practice had made revaluation an expected characteristic of the genre.

The problem arises when that revaluation is conducted while nevertheless imitating a certain set of events—battles, a night raid, a descent to the underworld—that Virgil's imitative practice also implied were essential to the genre. Earlier I cited Thomas Greene's formulation of this generic requirement: "really to count," he says, "the new work would have to look like the *Aeneid*"; its narratives would have to include a particular set of actions. But Milton seems to have decided that it was not so important for his epic to look like the *Aeneid* as to sound like the *Iliad*. He breaks with Virgil in terms of the "method of imitation" that Virgil's practice had suggested was proper to epic composition. Milton imitates Homer (and other writers) primarily at the level of the phrase rather than of the episode—suggesting by this practice that what makes a particular poem an epic is not a conventional set of episodes, but a particular stylistic or aesthetic effect, one in which wonder combines with familiarity.

Though I will argue that Milton reconciled Christian and classical elements differently than Steadman and Kates claim he did, I follow them in believing that it is the theory of epic expounded in Tasso's *Discourses on the Heroic Poem* and exemplified in *Jerusalem Delivered* that suggested to Milton this shift in the level of imitation. The inquiry Tasso conducted in the opening book of *Discourses on the Heroic Poem* into the effect proper to heroic poetry (wonder) opened the possibility of moving beyond a conception of epic based on a particular set of events. Latent in Tasso's claim that the effect proper to epic is to arouse wonder is the possibility that something other than the traditional epic episodes might arouse that wonder. In his theorizing, at least, Tasso never realizes this latent possibility. One can see, even in the passage in which he mentions the epic effect of wonder, that he considers a particular set of actions (here emphasized by italics) to be the source of that effect:

> to move wonder fits no kind of poetry so much as epic: so
> Aristotle teaches, and Homer himself in *Hector's flight*; for
> the wonder that almost stuns us as we see *one man alone*

dismaying an entire army with his threats and gestures would be inappropriate to tragedy, yet makes the epic poem marvellous. Nor would *the death of Hector* be appropriate on stage....Nor would *the metamorphosis of Cadmus into a serpent*...nor *that of Arethusa, or the nymphs transformed into ships* in Virgil.[9]

The events narrated in the poem are, in Tasso's theory, what arouses wonder.

In his poetic practice, however, Tasso to some extent deviates from Virgil's imitative method. True, Tasso frequently imitates the episodes of previous epic writers. For example, Clorinda and Argantes's night raid on the Christian troops is modeled on the Nisus and Euryalus episode in the ninth book of the *Aeneid* (which in turn is modeled on the Doloneia narrated in the tenth book of the *Iliad*). Likewise, behind the episode in which Tancred chops into a tree and finds that it houses his beloved Clorinda stands the episode in the third book of the *Aeneid* in which Aeneas pulls branches off a myrtle, which eventually reveals itself to be his fellow Trojan Polydorus.

But there is another type of imitation operative in Tasso's epic as well that concerns less the events narrated in the epic than the articulation of the epic narrative. When, for instance, Tasso begins his narration of a new action with the line, "But when the new dawn appeared in the sky," he is echoing the familiar Homeric transition line, "when the young dawn showed again with her rosy fingers."[10] Tasso does not intend that we compare the situation he describes with some similar situation in the Homeric poems; in fact, such a comparison would be impossible since Homer uses this line 22 times in his two epics, in a variety of situations.[11] The line is simply a customary way in an epic of describing a new day and leading into a new action. Into this same category of epic articulation falls the moment when the narrator claims, "And had it not been that it was not the day that God had written in his eternal decrees, this had been perhaps the

day that the invincible host arrived at the end of its holy labors"
(*JD* 7.114); this repeats the general syntax of a number of Homer's
"and now...had not" statements.[12]

To put the matter crudely, one might say that Virgil fragmented
the Homeric epics into a set of episodes that he then redistributed
(and romanized) to form his own heroic poem. Tasso follows this
practice but also in some cases fragments his sources even more
finely, imitating as much the manner of articulating an epic as the
particular episodes from an epic (a practice that allows for the whole
of his poem to be recognizably epic, even where strict episodic imitation might have threatened the Christian revaluation he was con-
ducting). Milton follows his precursors and extends their practice; he
fragments even more finely—down to the level of the phrase—and
in so doing radically reconceives the essential properties of the epic.

Phrasal Imitation

Like Tasso, Milton appropriates the narrative syntax of classical epic; indeed, he imitates some of the same passages Tasso had.
The opening of book 6 of *Paradise Lost* describes "Morn...with
rosy hand"—a direct imitation of Homer's customary method of
describing a new day. Milton's narrator three times interrupts his
story with an "and now...had not" comment (*PL* 2.722, 4.990,
6.669) to reveal how events might have gone if something else had
not happened. The line that describes Adam, Eve, and Raphael
finishing their meal—"Thus when with meats and drinks they
had suffic'd" (*PL* 5.451)—echoes a line frequently used by Homer
to close off the description of a sacrificial meal: αὐτὰρ ἐπεὶ πόσιος
καὶ ἐδητύος ἐξ ἔρον ἔντο ("But when they had put aside desire of
drink and of meat") (*Iliad* 1.469, e.g.).

Besides such appropriations of narrative syntax, though, there
is in *Paradise Lost* another species of allusion that has been largely
neglected in previous studies of Milton's relation to his precursors, neglected due to the hermeneutic bias of traditional allusion

study. In Porter's taxonomy of allusive types, these would be reminiscences, brief passages in Milton's poem that echo previous
texts, but not in order to enhance or qualify the meaning of his
own poem.[13] This is partly a matter of length; the allusions I have
in mind are usually one line or perhaps just a few words—reprises
that have a familiar ring, but are too brief fully to call to mind
their spur. Length, though, is not the only criterion, for allusions
often serve as a sort of poetic shorthand through which a poet can
summon up, with just a familiar word or two, not only the spur
on which his or her own reprise is based, but the larger context in
which that spur originally appeared. For example, the single word
man in the opening line of *Paradise Lost* recalls the *vir* in the
opening line of the *Aeneid* and its source, the ανηρ in the opening
line of the *Odyssey*. The context this allusion activates for comparison with Milton's epic is arguably the whole of Homer's and
Virgil's poems, since the spur announces that Milton's epic will
offer a new perspective on what it is to be human.

More important than length, then, for the phrasal allusions I
wish to discuss is their relative lack of local significance; it is in
many cases difficult to establish a meaning for one of Milton's
allusions. In his initial description of Eden, for instance, Milton
speaks of a profusion of flowers "where the morning Sun first
warmly smote / The open field" (*PL* 4.244–45). This line is almost
an exact translation of a line that appears once in the *Iliad* and
once in the *Odyssey*—"Now the sun of a new day struck on the
ploughlands" (*Iliad* 7.421; *Odyssey* 19.433). Even if the initial
interpretive problem could be solved (even if, that is, one could
determine to which instance of this Homeric formula Milton
alludes), neither context would seem significantly to intersect
with the picture that Milton is here painting of Eden. In the *Iliad*,
this line marks the beginning of a day of truce, in which the
Greeks and Trojans have agreed not to fight, so that each side can
retrieve its dead soldiers from the battlefield. In the *Odyssey*, the
line appears in the nurse Eurykleia's account of how Odysseus
received the scar on his thigh. Milton is, I think, oblivious
to the Homeric contexts of the image and to the way those con-

texts might modify the meaning of his text; he aims instead simply to reproduce an impressive image of bright sunshine.

The same sort of purely aesthetic impulse seems to underlie other allusions. Milton describes the construction of Pandaemonium as follows: "Anon out of the earth a Fabrick huge / Rose like an Exhalation" (*PL* 1.710–11). Editors have noted here an echo of a line in the first book of the *Iliad* that describes Thetis emerging from the sea: καρπαλίμως δ᾽ ἀνέδυ πολιῆς ἁλὸς ἠΰτ᾽ ὀμίχλη ("Quickly she rose from the grey sea like a mist") (*Iliad* 1.359). There is, as far as I can tell, no way in which knowing the original context enhances our understanding of the line; the situations are neither similar, nor meaningfully dissimilar.[14] Milton has simply borrowed a striking image and based the general movement of his line on that of Homer. Many of Milton's allusions, then (to Homer and other authors), seem designed merely to be reminiscent of epic diction rather than to prompt the interpretive efforts so characteristic of most allusion study.

In claiming that some of Milton's allusions carry little or no meaning, I realize I must be careful. As detailed in chapter 1, when a reader encounters a reprise modeled on a spur in the work of some earlier author, it tends to prompt a comparison between the context of that spur and the context of the reprise. There is nothing to limit how large a context surrounding the spur might be mined for details corresponding to elements in the context of the reprise; moreover, such details can lend significance either through similarity or contrast. To illustrate how profusely allusions tend to generate meaning, I will consider at some length a reading by John Shawcross of an allusion to Homer in book 4 of *Paradise Lost*. He notes that the following simile describing the troop of guardian angels is modeled on one from book 2 of the *Iliad*:

> [They] began to hemm [Satan] round
> With ported Spears, as thick as when a field
> Of *Ceres* ripe for harvest waving bends
> Her bearded Grove of ears, which way the wind
> Swayes them.   (4.979–85)

The comparison of warriors all leaning in one direction is borrowed from a simile describing the Greek troops' movements when Agamemnon encourages them to depart the Trojan battlefield: "As when the west wind moves across the grain deep standing, / boisterously, and shakes and sweeps it till the tassels lean, so / all of that assembly was shaken" (2.147–49).[15] Shawcross interprets the allusion as an "ironic description of the steadfastness toward duty which the guardian angels exhibit, for it is not the angels who flee or are even tempted to flee, but rather Satan."[16]

Observe the two interpretive moves here. First, if the fleeing Greeks are to be associated with the stalwart angels, it must be by contrast. And second, the Homeric detail of fleeing is associated with something else (namely Satan) in the immediate context of Milton's reprise. These interpretive procedures continue. Shawcross remarks of the Greek warriors, "Their return, Homer says, would have been against the will of fate." He is referencing a verse that appears five lines after the grain simile: "Then for the Argives a homecoming beyond fate might have / been accomplished" (2.155–56). Shawcross connects this with the Miltonic situation by associating the line with the loyal angels, but again asserting that the core meaning of the Greek verse functions through contrast: "Their opposition to Satan, the further context of the Greek epic implies, is a part of God's will." He then once more broadens the Homeric context relevant to the Miltonic line by recalling that the next narrative development in book 2 is for Athena to prompt Odysseus to stem the Argive retreat. This reversal, in his reading, applies (contrastingly) to Satan: "while the Greeks will be deterred by Athene (Wisdom) and will enter and conquer Troy, it is Satan who will return, reenter Eden, and conquer the first parents." Finally, the Miltonic context on which this allusion bears becomes the entirety of *Paradise Lost*, and the context for the spur extends beyond the *Iliad* to the Troy saga generally: "The ruse of the Trojan horse and the serpent's body is worthy of note as well."[17]

There is nothing implausible about Shawcross's interpretations; moreover, his mode of advancing his interpretation is typical of the analysis of allusions. But if verbal echoes can potentially bring along with them all of the details from extensive contexts, and if they can contribute meaning to the allusive text either by reinforcing through similarity or ironizing through contrast, then it would be hard to imagine the textual echo that could not be made to mean *something*. While it is true that one of the objections most frequently leveled against studies of allusions is that the critic has made the allusion under examination carry more meaning than it can legitimately shoulder, nevertheless, for me to argue that Milton's allusions have no meaning—may seem to be going too far in the opposite direction. While many allusions have no local significance, such allusions nevertheless have an aggregate effect.

On his journey from hell to Eden, Satan encounters Chaos, who describes how the earth is linked to heaven by a golden chain (*PL.* 2.1005–07). On reading about a golden chain hanging from heaven, readers familiar with the *Iliad* are likely to recall the moment in Homer's epic when Zeus boasts of his superiority over the combined might of all the other gods:

> Let down out of the sky a cord of gold; lay hold of it
> all you who are gods and all who are goddesses, yet not
> even so can you drag Zeus from the sky to the ground.
> . . . .
>
> So much stronger am I than the gods, and stronger than
> mortals.   (*Iliad* 8.19–21, 27)

Knowing the Homeric passage does little to enrich, enhance, or qualify (to use terms ubiquitous in hermeneutic study of allusion) the meaning of Milton's poem. In describing the golden chain, Chaos refers to what is presumably an actual feature of the physical universe, while Zeus's reference is purely hypothetical. The defiant Olympians at the one end of Homer's golden chain resemble the earth as little as the boastful Zeus at the other end resembles the Christian God. Of course, it is true that allusions may have their significance through contrast—the context of the spur can either reinforce the meaning of the reprise or subvert it—so a dissimilarity can be as significant as a resemblance. For instance, the opening to book 8 of *Paradise Lost:* "The Angel ended and in Adams Eare / So Charming left his voice, that he a while / Thought him still speaking," is reminiscent of the description in book 2 of the *Iliad* that depicts Agamemnon waking from the delusive dream Zeus has sent to him: "Agamemnon awoke from sleep, the divine voice drifting / around him" (41). Milton undoubtedly views Raphael's discourse as the antithesis of the delusive dream Zeus sends to Agamemnon.

The allusion, then, is so manifestly inappropriate as to be highly appropriate—as a foil. Since allusions can thus have their meaning through contrast as well as congruity, one might argue that the golden chain allusion works in that way. The Christian God, in such an interpretation, would gain in dignity by being compared to the boastful Zeus, and the obedience of the newly created world, or more precisely its pair of human occupants, would appear the more vividly due to the contrast with the defiant Olympians at the other end of Homer's chain. Again, given the complexity of both the source text and the alluding text and the possibility of an allusion having meaning either through similarity or dissimilarity, it would be a rare instance in which some set of details in the two passages could not be seen (or made) meaningfully to correspond. But most readers would regard as strained the hypothetical interpretation of the golden-chain allusion mentioned above. In a phrase that Charles Martindale uses to dismiss one of Blessington's interpretations, "it smacks of the study" rather than of the direct experience of reading.[18]

In claiming that certain of Milton's allusions are meaningless, I am not invoking the deconstructive tenet that determinate meaning is endlessly deferred. I am making the rather more modest claim that for a significant number of the textual echoes in *Paradise Lost,* while it may not be impossible for a reader to determine some way in which the source enriches the meaning of the alluding passage, such significance either does not come readily to mind or exists among so many seemingly noncorresponding details as to emerge only through elaborate scholarly archeology.

Though none of them has pursued the issue, other critics have observed the relative meaninglessness of many of Milton's allusions. Martin Mueller comments, "Milton's technique of allusion is peculiarly fragmentary compared with Virgil's," and "as a result the allusion rarely has any structural significance." David Masson puts it this way: "Original as it is, original in its entire conception, and in every portion and passage, the poem is yet full of flakes—we can express it no otherwise—full of flakes from all that is greatest in preceding literature." Charles Martindale, like Mueller, finds a fundamental difference in the way that Virgil and Milton allude: "We can perceive behind Virgil's words the continual ghostly presence of the plot of the *Iliad* and *Odyssey,* and may be encouraged to reflect on both differences and similarities. Milton's allusions sometimes work in this way, but it is doubtful whether this is so with the majority." And, as I have already mentioned, William Porter, in his book-length study of Milton's relation to his classical epic predecessors, finds only a single meaningful allusion to Homer in all of *Paradise Lost.*[19]

Indeed, Martindale claims, "there are occasions on which we need positively to repress any knowledge of the original context."[20] An example might be found in book 3 of *Paradise Lost* when Milton says of the seven archangels that they "Bear [God's] swift errands over moist and dry, / O're Sea and Land" (652–53). In this, the archangels resemble Hera's horses that bear her "over hard land and water" (*Iliad* 14.307). To compare archangels to horses, even divine horses, would be demeaning, if not sacrilegious. We can feel certain that Milton did not want readers to examine the context of his source, but simply to be impressed by what is described in the line: a creature that can travel even over water.

Moreover, if the context must on occasion be repressed lest absurd meanings result, there are other instances in which it is unlikely that the context would even be recalled in the first place. For example, Milton says of Mulciber, "nor aught avail'd him now / To have built in Heav'n high Towrs; nor did he scape / By all his Engins" (*PL* 1.748–50). The neither-nor structure of this line seems to some commentators to recall Homer's description of the death of a Trojan named Skamandrios: "Artemis of the showering arrows could not now help him, / no, nor the long spearcasts in which he had been pre-eminent" (*Iliad* 5.53–54). But Skamandrios is by no means a major figure in the *Iliad*; Homer mentions him only this once, at the moment of his death. So there is no way in which his being likened to Mulciber helps to flesh out the personality of that devil. Moreover, the passage in question appears in a section of the poem that briefly describes the death of a number of soldiers as, one after another, they fall in battle. Homer takes care to relate a personal detail about each of the slain men, but there is little to make Skamandrios particularly memorable among them. It is doubtful that Milton expected even fit readers to recall the context of the passage that he imitates; he may not have remembered it himself. More likely he simply wanted to reproduce the rhetorical force of this particular line (this did not avail him, no, nor did that), and was indifferent to the context in which it originally occurred.

Under this category of allusions for which the context is unlikely to be recalled fall those allusions Milton makes to Homer's formulas. I have already noted one such allusion, when I showed how Milton's "the morning Sun first warmly smote / The open field" reproduces a line that occurs once in the *Iliad* and once in the *Odyssey*. Likewise, when Milton calls Moloch "Scepter'd King," he alludes to a Homeric phrase that occurs six times in the two epics.[21] When Satan proposes his plan that someone go to earth and attempt to corrupt humankind, Milton says of the fallen angels that "all sat mute"; a response of this nature — "all of them stayed stricken to silence" — is something that occurs 15 times in

Homer's epics.[22] And the following description of Satan, "under Browes / Of dauntless courage, and considerate Pride / Waiting revenge: cruel his eye" (*PL* 1.602–04), seems to owe something to Homer's ὑπόδρα ἰδών ("looking from under his brows"), which occurs 26 times in the two epics.[23] Surely, in instances such as this, it is impossible to ask what the source contributes to the alluding passage, for it is impossible to know which of several passages is the source.[24]

In Milton's allusions to Homer, then, there are a number of factors that militate against our efforts to assign meaning: either there is no single spur with which we can connect the reprise; or, if there is, it is not likely to be recalled even by a learned reader; or else the immediate context of the spur seems to provide no readily discernible points of comparison or contrast with the immediate context of the reprise. By what is admittedly my own subjective count, in nearly half of the cases in which Milton's words recall those of Homer, one or more of these factors interferes with treating the allusion as an occasion for interpretation.

The Aesthetic Effect of "Meaningless" Allusions

Because of the exclusively hermeneutic focus of most allusion study, previous scholars, when they have mentioned such allusions at all, have tended to dismiss them as not worthy of much attention. I believe, however, that these "meaningless" allusions are by no means insignificant. Their significance lies in their aggregate effect, which is to reproduce in a written epic the aesthetic effect of the formulaic diction in which oral epics like those of Homer are composed.

The effect of Homer's formulaic diction is a complex one. Milman Parry describes the impact of Homer's mode of composition: "[Homer's audience] quickly learned not to look for any particularized meaning. They were so *familiar* with the fact that the noun-epithet combination is no more than a *heroic* mode of expressing a noun that all they expected to find in the epithet was an element ennobling the style."²⁵ The diction is perceived by the audience as simultaneously heroic and familiar, elevated and everyday.

In his expansion of Parry's theory of formulaic diction, Albert Lord prints the opening of the *Iliad* with solid and dashed lines under each verse to show the degree of formularity:

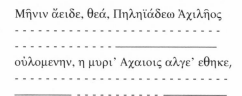

Μῆνιν ἄειδε, θεά, Πηληϊάδεω Ἀχιλῆος

οὐλομενην, η μυρι' Αχαιοις αλγε' εθηκε,

In Parry's markings, the solid underlines designate phrases that are attested verbatim elsewhere in the existing corpus of ancient Greek dactylic hexameter verse (formulas)—so that, for instance, the exact phrase Πηληϊάδεω Ἀχιλῆος also appears in the *Iliad* at 1.322, 9.166, and five other times in Homer's epics. The dotted lines designate phrases that are formulaic; verses using some of the same elements as other verses in the corpus. Lord reproduces the opening 15 lines of the *Iliad* to show that 90 percent of the phrases in that passage are either full-fledged formulas or at least formulaic.²⁶ Something similar might be done with the densely allusive passages from *Paradise Lost*. Consider a passage from Milton's epic with content similar to the passage from Homer chosen by Lord, mighty warriors being cast into the underworld:

> <u>Nine days they fell</u>; confounded *Chaos* <u>roard</u>,
> And felt tenfold confusion in thir fall
> Through his wilde Anarchie, so huge a rout
> Incumberd him with ruin: <u>Hell at last</u>
> <u>Yawning receavd</u> them whole, and on them clos'd,
> Hell, thir fit habitation fraught with <u>fire</u>
> <u>Unquenchable, the house of woe and paine</u>.   (*PL* 6.871–77)

The nine-day fall and roaring of Chaos are from Hesiod's *Theogony* (722, 679); the description of hell as a mouth that swallows the falling angels is from Isaiah 5:14, and the word *yawning* in particular is drawn from Phineas Fletcher's *Purple Island* (7.45.7); the "fire unquenchable" is from Mark 9:43; the phrase "house of woe and paine" is based on a verse in Fairfax's translation of Tasso's *Gerusalemme liberata* (9.59.6). The passage from Masson quoted earlier as a recognition of the meaninglessness of many of Milton's allusions is apposite here again. *Paradise Lost* is not only "full of *flakes* from all that is greatest in preceding literature"; it is *full* of such flakes.[27] Milton's epic is a sort of cento of the preceding Western tradition of literature. While the *content* of both Homer and Milton's passages here is destruction of unprecedented magnitude, the *phraseology* through which that destruction is in both cases conveyed is, precisely (if paradoxically), precedented.

We should not regard this paradoxical effect as simply an accident of Homer's oral mode of composition and of Milton's immense learning. At least one important theorist of the heroic poem, Tasso, saw precisely such a mix of the wondrous and the familiar as a defining characteristic of the genre. The proper epic effect, Tasso argues, is to arouse wonder or admiration. Yet the epic is also marked by a concern for verisimilitude. In his *Discourses on the Heroic Poem*, Tasso never explicitly addresses the fact that these two values—*meraviglia* and *verisimilitudine*—oppose one another. In practice, according to Kates, he is "able to reconcile what look like opposing elements in epic tradition, the 'verisimilar' and the 'marvelous.' By attributing the supernatural occurrences to God, the angels, devils and other figures believed by Christians to possess miraculous powers, the poet can write a poem that includes both elements and yet never sacrifices verisimilitude."[28] But Tasso's method of reconciling these opposing tendencies at the level of the episode means that he gets to exploit their fruitful tension only on the relatively rare occasions on which he describes a miracle, for that is the only time when an action can be at once marvelous and verisimilar.

Milton's approach differs from that of Tasso and allows a more frequent and complete interpenetration of the wondrous and the familiar. He describes marvelous events, events arguably more marvelous than anything in *Jerusalem Delivered*. But the allusive density of his verse ensures that the language in which he describes his marvels consistently sounds at least vaguely familiar—even as Homer, while describing the wondrous feats of the soldiers who fought at Troy, does so in phrases that his audience has repeatedly heard before. As astonishing as may be the appearance—"Gloomie as Night"—of the Son on the third day of the war in heaven, that marvel feels all the more terrifyingly real by recalling Hector breaking the Greek wall and Apollo visiting a plague on the Achaeans (*PL* 6.832; *Iliad* 12.462–63, 1.47).

The canonicity of *Paradise Lost* is partly a result of Milton's having supplied a desideratum that literary theorists of his era hoped would validate the very notion of a "Renaissance." Milton's success in filling the canonical slot of "Christian epic" formulated by poetic theorists of his day results, I believe, from his providing that mix of the familiar and the marvelous those theorists regarded as proper to epic, but locating them not in a particular set of actions—

> the wrauth
> Of Stern *Achilles* on his Foe pursu'd
> Thrice Fugitive about *Troy* Wall; or rage
> Of *Turnus* for *Lavinia* disespous'd
> Or *Neptun's* ire or *Juno's*, that so long
> Perplex'd the *Greek* and *Cytherea's* Son   (*PL* 9.13–19)

—but in what he, in the very next line, requests that his Celestial Patroness grant him: an "answerable style."

FOUR

"From the First"

Conceptions of Origins and Their Consequences

One of the primary discursive mechanisms by which *Paradise Lost* was established and has been maintained in the literary canon is the notion of originality. At least as early as 1704, in John Dennis's *Grounds of Criticism in Poetry*, *Paradise Lost* was being canonized on the basis of its being "an Original Poem; that is to say, a Poem that should have his own Thoughts, his own Images, and his own Spirit."[1] Later in the eighteenth century, Samuel Johnson similarly praised Milton's originality (though with some reservation): "The highest praise of genius is original invention. Milton cannot be said to have contrived the structure of an epick poem, and therefore owes reverence to that vigor and amplitude of mind to which all generations must be indebted for the art of poetical narration.... But of all the borrowers from Homer Milton

93

is perhaps the least indebted."[2] Moreover, Johnson links the value of *Paradise Lost*, what we would call its canonical status, to this quality of originality by observing that Milton's "work is not the *greatest* of heroic poems, only because it is not the *first*."[3] The quality of originality, moreover, continues to this day to play a role in maintaining Milton's canonical status. Barbara Lewalski's recent biography of Milton, for example, counts "stunning originality" as one of the "constants in Milton's poetry."[4]

In this chapter, I argue that Milton anticipated the role that the term *original* would play in the canonization of his epic, and that he did so in part by observing the way in which Homer's epics were being canonically reproduced in his own day. I argue further that Milton's conception of originality—developed at a time when the word *original* was undergoing a semantic shift, and participating in both the established and emerging senses of the term—might help us better conceptualize the position Milton saw his epic as inhabiting within the epic tradition.

Origins

However instrumental the concept of originality may have been in the process by which *Paradise Lost* initially achieved and has since maintained its canonical status, we must recognize that the concept of originality is rich and complex, that the meaning of the word *original* has been historically variable, and that it was in Milton's day only just beginning to acquire the specific shade of meaning by which it has since come to serve as a laudatory term within literary criticism. The *OED*'s earliest witness for the word *original* in the sense of "not imitated from another" is the preface to John Dryden's 1700 *Fables Ancient and Modern*, where he announces that to his imitations of Homer, Ovid, and Boccaccio he has "added some Original papers of [his] own." Of course, our earliest witness of a term's use is only rarely that term's first actual use. And in this instance, one can be more certain than usual that Dryden is not here coining this sense of the term; since the word appears in the same sense in the subtitle of his book (*Translated into Verse, from Homer, Ovid, Boccace and Chaucer: With Original Poems*), Dryden obviously did not feel that he needed any context in order to make this sense of the term clear, as he likely would have felt had he thought he was advancing a new sense for the word *original*. So, rather than assigning the new sense of the word *original* to 1700, we should perhaps say, more generally, that in the later seventeenth century a new sense of the meaning of originality was beginning to emerge.[5]

The previous dominant sense of the word *original* was "that from which something arises, proceeds, or is derived" (a sense that is still current, for example, in the "original" from which photocopies are made). Milton uses the word in this sense when, for example, Beelzebub predicts that future generations of human-kind will curse Adam and Eve as their "frail originals" (2.375). We should mark, though, that the sense attested in the Dryden quotation is not simply a slightly different shade of meaning accruing to an existing term. The sense of *original* that emerged in the later seventeenth century represents a diametrical reversal in the temporal perspective from which originality is viewed: the older sense of *original* regards an origin in connection with that which follows from it; the newer sense, in contrast with what preceded it.[6] We might associate this semantic shift with larger ideological shifts underway in the early modern period, particularly the shift in the grounds of human knowledge from a backward-looking respect for ancient authorities to a forward-looking focus on the accumulating results of scientific experimentation. David Quint's history of this concept, *Origin and Originality in Renaissance Literature*, links early modern authors' handling of the source topos to precisely such developments in Western intellectual history.[7]

Perhaps in part because of this instability in the meaning of the word *original* during the period in which he was composing his mature works, Milton was himself acutely interested in origins. Regina Schwartz characterizes him as "preoccupied with origins" and offers an extensive list of the moments of origin he treats in his writings: "the origin of the cosmos, the birth of his god, the birth of the first man and the first woman, the first utterance, the first interpretation, the first temptation, the first rebellion, the first home, and the first exile."[8] But (again perhaps because the composition of *Paradise Lost* straddles a period in which the meaning of originality was in flux), the understanding of origins manifest within the epic is complex.

Milton's epic figures origins as binary in nature: an event, the poem insists, is only an origin in conjunction with that which follows from it and repeats it. This unusual, and perhaps paradoxical, conception of origins underlies the major action of the poem, for in *Paradise Lost* the "original sin" is emphatically not the first transgression, Eve's, but the first two transgressions: Eve's eating of the forbidden fruit *together with* Adam's repetition of her action. The language of the passage in which Milton describes Adam's fatal trespass provocatively underscores the binary nature of the initial sin. When Adam ate of the forbidden fruit, we are told, Earth trembled and the sky "wept at compleating of the mortal Sin / Original" (*PL* 9.1003–04). If we ordinarily understand an origin as the abrupt single instant when something differs markedly from what had preceded it, then to figure an origin as susceptible to, or even requiring, *completion* represents an unconventional formulation. To understand such a suggestion demands that one see an origin as a bifurcated occurrence, in which an earlier event brings about a later event (as Eve's disobedience does Adam's) but is nevertheless only properly an origin *in conjunction with* that later event.[9]

Milton's unconventional formulation of the concept of originality—a formulation that stresses that a second, repetitive act is necessary to fully constitute an origin—underlies many of the other origins depicted in the epic as well. Milton's handling of the origin of angelic disobedience commences with a verbatim, but ironized, repetition of the line of titles with which the Father had begun the exaltation of the Son: "Thrones, Dominations, Princedoms, Vertues, Powers" (*PL* 5.601, 772). The plan to corrupt mankind originates with Beelzebub's *repetition* of "devilish Counsel, first devis'd / By *Satan* and in part propos'd" (2.379–80). Similarly, the origin of repentance is described in the famously repetitive passage closing book 10 that converts intention to action. Milton signals the importance of this formulation, in which it is only together with an imitative second action that an early action fully becomes an origin, with the pun in the opening line of the poem, where the word *fruit* suggests a relation between origin (fruit as a synecdoche for the initial sin) and consequence (in the word's punning sense of "results") so close as to suggest that consequence partly constitutes origin.

An image from geometry—that of the ray—might help us to characterize Milton's binary conception of origins as emphasizing both the point of origin and some subsequent related moment. Just as, in Euclidian geometry, a ray is determined by two points, the origin and one other point along its length, so too, in Milton's vision, are the consequences that follow from a particular event essential to that earlier event's being an origin—and essential as well to determining the trajectory that the remainder of the consequences will follow: the "sin / Original" becomes Original Sin, the congenital depravity of all of Adam and Eve's offspring. By comparison with the pre-Enlightenment meaning of *original*, which stresses that which follows from an origin, and the post-Enlightenment meaning, which stresses the radical departure from what had preceded, Milton's conception is evenly balanced between the two alternatives.

Milton's handling of origins in his epic suggests, then, that he was attuned on some level to the sense of the term *original* emerging in the later seventeenth century. And if I am correct that Milton anticipated the role the newer meaning was to have in the evaluation and canonization of literary works, that might be at least in part a result of his attention to how Homer was being canonically reproduced in the mid-seventeenth century, especially the way in which critics conceived Homer's status relative to Virgil.

Homeric Invention and Virgilian Refinement

To give a rough sense of the change in Homer's canonical status relative to Virgil, we might compare the views of Giulio Cesare Scaliger and Samuel Johnson, the foremost critics of a century before and a century after *Paradise Lost*, respectively. Scaliger devotes the fifth book of his 1561 *Poetics* to a comparison between Greek authors and the Latin authors who imitated them. By far the longest section of this book, and indeed of the entire treatise, is an examination of passages from the *Aeneid* modeled on those in Homer's two epics. That comparison is prefaced by the following general observation:

> Homeri ingenium maximum: ars eiusmodi, ut eam potius invenisse, quam excoluisse vidatur.... Virgilius vero artem ab eo rudem acceptam lectioris naturae studiis, atque judicio ad summum extulit fatigium perfectionis. Quodque perpaucis datum est, multa detrahendo fecit auctiorem. Neque enim in mole, frequentiane orationis, sed in castitate atq; frugalitate magnitudo constituta est.
>
> [Homer's greatest talent is an art of such a kind as rather to invent something than to improve it.... Virgil truly with more select study of nature and with judgment carried forward the rude art he had received from Homer to the highest summit of perfection. By purging many things, he augmented what he had been given. For, not in buildings, true, but in literary works, as in personal character, frugality frequently constitutes magnificence.][10]

One way of viewing the merit of an earlier author relative to a later author is to suggest that the later author improves what is crudely expressed by his predecessor; here, in part by purging (*detrahendo*), Virgil refines Homer's crude inventions (*inuenisse*). By contrast, as we have seen, Johnson states flatly that "the highest praise of genius is original invention" and reveres "that vigor and amplitude of mind to which all generations must be indebted for the art of poetical narration"; for him, the most artistically meritorious quality is clearly originality rather than refinement.

For both Scaliger and Johnson, the literary-historical test case for the relative merits of invention and improvement is Homer and his successors in epic. In his lifetime, Milton could have discerned the shift from a Scaligerian preference for Virgilian refinement to a Johnsonian preference for Homeric originality. As late as Spenser, Scaliger's view seems to have predominated. When, in the "Letter to Raleigh" accompanying the *Faerie Queene,* Spenser speaks of how "Homer...in the Persons of Agamemnon and Ulysses hath ensampled a good governour and a vertuous man, the one in his Ilias, the other in his Odysseis" and how Virgil's "like intention was to do in the person of Aeneas," he seems to be echoing a passage in Scaliger that makes this conflation of qualities in a single hero a sign of Virgil's superiority.[11] But just 20 years later, George Chapman opens the preface to his 1611 translation of the *Iliad* with the following claim: "Of all books extant in all kinds, Homer is the first and best. No one before his, Josephus affirmes, nor before him, saith Velleius Paterculus, was there any whom he imitated, nor after him any that could imitate him."[12]

The highlighted tributes of Josephus and Velleius Paterculus link Homer's superiority to (if it is not yet called his "originality") his anteriority.[13] Fifty years further on, at the time Milton was composing *Paradise Lost,* this respect for Homer's originality is evident, for example, in how James Duport explains his motives for compiling *Homeri gnomologia.* He finds it shameful that no one has previously collected Homer's sententia, especially since Sophocles, Euripides, Plato, Demosthenes, and other Greek writers (not to mention the Romans) "omnes ex fontibus Homericis suos hortos irrigarunt" (all watered their own gardens from the Homeric spring).[14]

Far from regarding Homer as Scaliger had, as an inventive but crude primitive refined by later authors like Virgil, seventeenth century critics were coming to regard Homer as possessing an originary plenitude merely reappropriated by later authors. Milton himself, even from his Cambridge years, regarded Homer's primacy in a positive light. In Prolusion 6, he speaks of how "first of all Homer appears, that rising sun and morning star of more refined literature, with whom all learning like a twin was born" (CM 12:218). (And interestingly, given the verbal context within which I have been considering this matter, the Latin of the prolusion uses the word that is the root for *original:* "primus omnium occurrit Homerus ille *oriens,* & Lucifer cultioris literaturae"; emphasis added). In this connection, it is perhaps also significant that one of the Italian theorists Milton singles out in *Of Education* as having provided instruction in "the sublime art" of poetics is Castelvetro, whose *Poetica d'Aristotele vulgarizzata e sposta* was remarkable among Renaissance treatises for the emphasis it put on originality: "the poet is essentially an inventor, and a writer without invention is no poet."[15]

Indeed, Milton places *Paradise Lost* in alignment with Homeric originality rather than Virgilian refinement in part by alluding to passages that in Scaliger's *Poetics* are cited to illustrate the superiority of Virgil over Homer, and then, in his own allusion to both poets, imitating Homer more closely. For example, Scaliger considers the storms stirred up by Poseidon in the *Odyssey*, book 5, and by Aeolus in the *Aeneid*, book 1. The Homeric spur runs as follows:

> [Poseidon] pulled all the clouds together, in both hands gripping
> the trident and staggered the sea, and let loose all the storm
>   blasts
> of all the winds together, and huddled under the cloud scuds
> land alike and the great water. Night sprang from heaven.
> East Wind and South Wind clashed together, and the bitter
>   blown West Wind
> and the North Wind born in the bright air rolled up a heavy sea.
>   (*Odyssey* 5.291–96)

Scaliger calls this "divine language" but then observes that it is an "imperfect description of a tempest."[16] Virgil's imitation of this passage in the description of the storm that drives Aeneas to Carthage has the east and south and southwest winds together (*creber*) lash up waves and drive them to shore, a description that Scaliger finds more effective because it omits Homer's inaccurate epithet calling Zephyr stormy — "the Zephyr is not a violent wind"—and the confusion of calling Boreas "born in the bright air" (αἰθρηγενενέτης) in the context of a scene just described as cloudy. Milton's imitation of this storm passage comes in book 10, when he describes the effects on the natural world of Adam and Eve's sin:

> now from the North
> Of *Norumbega,* and the *Samoed* shoar
> Bursting their brazen Dungeon, armd with ice
> And snow and haile and stormie gust and flaw,
> *Boreas,* and *Caecias* and *Argestes* loud
> And *Thrascias* rend the Woods and Seas upturn;
> With adverse blasts up-turns them from the South
> *Notus* and *Afer* black with thundrous clouds
> From *Serraliona;* thwart of these as fierce
> Forth rush the Levant and the *Ponent* Windes
> *Eurus* and *Zephir,* with thir lateral noise,
> *Sirocco,* and *Libecchio.*   (*PL* 10.695–706)

The most striking change Milton makes, of course, is to multiply the number of winds mentioned, from Virgil's three and Homer's four to his own ten. So in that regard, the Miltonic passage is an instance of epic topping. But at the same time, in broad conception, Milton returns from the Virgilian accuracy of having three winds operate together to turn up massive waves to the Homeric "divina...oratio" of having the mentioned winds "clash" against one another; the language of his own passage ("adverse," "thwart," "lateral") puts the emphasis on the violent encounter of the various winds. Indeed, his description of the northern winds as "armed with ice and snow and haile and stormie gust and flaw" almost seems a direct answer to Scaliger's quibble that an either-born Boreas has no place in a cloudy storm-scene, enumerating as it does forms of meteorological menace appropriate to northern winds and compatible with dark storm clouds.

Scaliger next focuses on Odysseus's and Aeneas's reactions to the storm, described in passages I examined in chapter 1, where knees relax and hearts melt. For Scaliger, in the Virgilian imitation of this scene, "How much more expressive are the words of Aeneas, which, by *being directed to the gods* and animated with fitting gesture, seem alive with feeling."[17] But again, regarding the detail on which Scaliger focuses, Milton's imitation follows Homer more closely than Virgil; Aeneas prays "lifting both hands to the stars," whereas Odysseus speaks "to his own great hearted spirit" and Adam also "*to himself*...inward silence broke" (*Aeneid* 1.93; *Odyssey* 5.298; *PL* 9.895; emphasis mine). In short, Milton targets precisely the passages Scaliger had used to illustrate Virgilian superiority and alludes to them in a way that, while topping both of his epic predecessors, nevertheless aligns him more closely with Homeric invention than Virgilian refinement. I would argue that this is a sign of Milton's intuition that canonical value was coming to be associated less with refinement and more with a quality that his age tended to call "invention" but that was coming to be called "originality."

Originality in Bloom

Canonical status, moreover, is not just a matter of the relative ranking assigned within particular periods to various candidates for the greatest epic, novel, or other work. A new literary work is not just one more contender in a weightlifting contest. As T. S. Eliot formulates it in "Tradition and the Individual Talent," an ambitious new literary work, by the relations it takes up with the preexisting body of canonical literary texts, implicitly alters our conception of that entire corpus of literary works:

> What happens when a new work of art is created is something that happens simultaneously to all the works of art which preceded it. The existing monuments form an ideal order among themselves, which is modified by the introduction of the new (the really new) work of art among them. The existing order is

complete before the new work arrives; for order to persist after the supervention of novelty, the *whole* existing order must be, if ever so slightly, altered; and so the relations, proportions, values of each work of art toward the whole are readjusted.[18]

The best way to envision this adjustment in the case of *Paradise Lost* (the readjustment Milton's epic implicitly effects on the Western literary tradition as it takes its place within that tradition) is through a deeper consideration of Milton's unusual conception of originality, which developed during a period in which a new sense of the word *original* was emerging. Milton's unique understanding of originality may be cast into relief by comparing it with that of Harold Bloom, the contemporary theorist of interpoetic relations for whom the concept of originality is most crucial, and a critic for whom Milton is a pivotal (yet vexing) figure.

Readers might have expected that Bloom would figure more prominently in my consideration of Milton's allusions to Homer. After all, he is the poststructuralist critic who most directly focuses on the issue of interpoetic relationships. But by his own pronouncements, Bloom's theory of the "anxiety of influence" turns out to have little to offer to a study of the relation between Milton and one of his major precursors, at least insofar as that relationship manifests itself in the kind of phraseological appropriations on which I have focused. For just as Kristeva attempts to distinguish her concept of intertextuality from "banal" misunderstandings that would make the term essentially synonymous with allusion, so too Bloom stresses that his understanding of poetic influence has little or nothing in common with traditional forms of connection between literary texts: "the profundities of poetic influence cannot be reduced to source-study, to the history of ideas, to the patterning of images."[19] Instead, "criticism is the art of knowing the *hidden* roads that go from poem to poem" (*Anxiety* 96; emphasis added). How little his understanding of poetic influence depends on discernible phraseological connections is evident from Bloom's claim that, in his "antithetical criticism . . . the meaning of a poem can only be . . . another poem . . . by an indubitable precursor, even if the ephebe *never read* that poem. Source study is wholly irrelevant here" (*Anxiety*, 70).

Accordingly, although Bloom's theory is focused on interpoetic relationships, it has little direct bearing on the conception of allusion developed in this study, which has focused on the relationship between Milton and Homer as that relationship can be characterized from Milton's phraseological adaptations of his predecessor. But with regard to broader forms of literary interrelation (interpoetic rivalry, tradition), Bloom's theory *is* relevant, particularly in how it casts into relief the concept of originality, which has been so crucial to the canonization of *Paradise Lost*.

The concept of originality is, of course, fundamental to much literary analysis, particularly the construction of literary and cultural histories. And the almost exclusively honorific force of the term *original* ensures that it functions as a mechanism in the canonization of almost every text that enters the literary canon. But the concept of originality, as I hope I have shown, is rich and complex, and the meaning of the word *original* has been historically variable. An origin can be understood either in relation to the antecedents from which it deviates, or in relation to the consequences that follow from it, or in terms of its own singularity. When Bloom, to whom the concept of origins is probably more important than to any other modern critic, articulates his understanding of the Western literary tradition, the form that history takes is determined in part by the understanding of origins and originality that underlies his literary theorizing. And the impact of his conception of origins on his sense of literary history is in fact nowhere more clear than in his treatment of Milton, a figure Bloom confesses that he finds particularly difficult to account for. I will argue that Bloom's difficulty arises from the historical boundedness of the conception of originality he adopts, and that by adopting an understanding closer to Milton's own—developed during an era in which the adjective *original* was undergoing a semantic shift, in which the meaning "not imitated from another" was emerging and gaining emphasis relative to the older meaning, "that from which something arises, proceeds, or is derived"—by adopting an understanding of *originality* sensitive to its meaning in Milton's day, we can provide a more nuanced account than Bloom does of the position Milton envisioned for *Paradise Lost* within the epic tradition.

The concept of originality was crucial within Bloom's famous influence tetralogy, and even in more recent work such as *The Western Canon*, it remains one element of the "amalgam" through which he believes a work breaks into the canon: "mastery of figurative language, originality, cognitive power, knowledge, exuberance of diction."[20] Bloom's treatment of the topic, in part because of the energy and extravagance with which it is articulated, illustrates vividly the connection between one's conception of origins and one's understanding of poetic tradition. One place where the connection between these two is especially apparent is in the chapter of *A Map of Misreading*, entitled "Milton and His Precursors," in which Bloom attempts to describe the place of *Paradise Lost* within the epic tradition. Yet in mapping the Western literary tradition (and not least in this chapter), Bloom experiences particular difficulty in accounting for the poetry of John Milton. This difficulty I attribute to the changes in the meaning of the word *original* between the latter half of the seventeenth century and the latter half of the twentieth.

There can be no mistaking the importance of Milton in Bloom's theory of poetic influence. One of Bloom's opening strategies in *The Anxiety of Influence* is to read *Paradise Lost* "as an allegory of the dilemma of the modern poet" (20). And elsewhere Bloom contends, "of the dozen or so major poetic influencers before this century [Milton] ranks as the great Inhibitor" and that "Milton is the central problem in any theory and history of poetic influence in English" (*Anxiety* 32, 33).

But the position Milton occupies in Bloom's theory, however privileged, is an unstable one, as the word *problem* in the preceding quotation might suggest. One sign of this instability is Bloom's vacillation on the question of whether or not his theory even applies to Milton. His declared purview is post-Enlightenment poetry, and on one occasion he claims that Milton "absorbed precursors with a gusto evidently precluding anxiety" (*Anxiety* 50). From such statements it would seem that the theory is not intended to apply to Milton. Yet on other occasions Bloom asserts the contrary: "Shakespeare belongs to the giant age before the flood, before the anxiety of influence became central to poetic consciousness" but Milton "with all his strength, yet had to struggle, subtly and crucially, with a major precursor in Spenser" (*Anxiety* 11). Indeed, so great is Bloom's uncertainty as to whether his theory applies to Milton or not, he can within the space of a single page argue that Milton "was incapable of suffering the anxiety of influence" and then go on to demonstrate the manner in which Spenser is Milton's precursor, his "Great Original" (*Anxiety* 34). Bloom seems eager to resolve this confusion; in *A Map of Misreading,* the second book in his influence tetralogy, he claims that he "would now assert only a difference in degree, rather than in kind, for influence-anxieties from Milton on."[21] But despite this attempt at clarification, the confusion remains. Milton, whose inclusion or exclusion was formerly unsettled, now occupies an ill-defined transitional position in Bloom's poetic history. And the ambiguity of Bloom's phrasing—"from Milton on"—leaves one wondering whether the change of which he is speaking occurs with or just after Milton.

A second indication of the unstable position Milton occupies in Bloom's theory is that even though, as I mentioned in the introduction of this chapter, Bloom typically excludes from his study obvious verbal echoes, claiming that they have "almost nothing to do with...poetic influence, in the sense [he] gives to it" and are suited only to "those carrion-eaters of scholarship, the source hunters," when he comes in *A Map of Misreading* to study Milton, it is precisely these obvious verbal echoes (of Homer, Virgil, Dante, Tasso, Spenser, and others) that he examines (*Map* 19, 17). Bloom admits the difficulty he has in accounting for Milton, confessing, in a later interview, "I am increasingly uncertain...as to whether we have a way of talking about what it is that Milton is actually doing in *Paradise Lost*. I reject completely the orthodox accounts, but I have not yet found one to replace them."[22]

Bloom's perplexity over Milton stems, I would argue, at least in part from his conception of origins and originality. The word *original* became a term of literary approbation in the eighteenth century and was given a special level of prominence in the evaluation of literary works by the Romantics. Perhaps Bloom's theory, unabashedly Romantic as it is in so many other ways, adopts a Romantic perspective on originality, and therefore one could argue that it is inapplicable to pre-Romantic literature. But the historical boundedness of Bloom's understanding of originality cannot be established simply by citing the Romantics' esteem for that quality, since writers have always sought to distinguish themselves from their predecessors, whether or not they have referred to such distinctiveness with the term *originality*. Carew, for example, praises Donne for his "fresh invention."[23] Milton reveals his desire to pursue "things unattempted yet in Prose and Rhime" (*PL* 1.16). And the Ariostian provenance of that line (besides demonstrating that Milton has no simplistic notion of originality and saw it as fully compatible with imitative appropriation) indicates that the desire was hardly new to Milton or Donne. If writers have always struggled to distinguish themselves in some way from their precursors, then Bloom's focus on originality need not, in itself, provide reason to regard his theory as limited to post-Enlightenment poets.

Despite the fact that authors have always aimed to differentiate their work from that of their precursors, the more historically informed consideration of the term *original* that I sketched above still can be of use in suggesting why Milton fits so uneasily in Bloom's theory. The term *original* has several distinct but interrelated senses, and Bloom strongly favors one of them, although not necessarily the one most appropriate to Milton.

In the evaluation of art, the word *original* is now customarily employed in contrast with the term *derivative*; we deem a given poem original when it seems fundamentally unlike earlier poems.

Bloom, true to his own imperative that "every word in a critic's vocabulary should swerve from inherited words," takes *original* in something closer to its root sense.[24] The anxiety of influence is aroused in a poet precisely because he or she wishes to be more than merely distinctive; desires to antedate predecessors, to be original in the sense of "initial, first, earliest," and not merely in the sense of "not derivative or dependent." "*Priority* in divination," Bloom maintains, "is crucial for every strong poet, lest he dwindle merely into a latecomer"; or again, "the commodity in which poets deal, their authority, their property, turns upon *priority*" (*Anxiety* 8, 64; emphasis mine). Such actual chronological priority is, of course, impossible to attain, but the revisionary ratios that Bloom enumerates are strategies of writing that make it *appear* possible; this is especially true of the ultimate ratio, *apophrades*, by which "the tyranny of time is almost overturned, and one can believe, for startled moments, that [historically late poets] are being *imitated by their ancestors*" (*Anxiety* 141).

Bloom, then, connects uniqueness of writing style with actual temporal priority along the trajectory of the word *originality*, which may now convey either of those meanings. This is a trajectory, however, that was unavailable before the eighteenth century because, as we have seen, the earliest witness for the word *original* in the sense of "not imitated from another" is in the preface to John Dryden's 1700 *Fables Ancient and Modern*, where he announces that to his imitations of Homer, Ovid, and Boccaccio he has "added some Original papers of [his] own."

So, Milton was undoubtedly able to conceive of that feature of artistic production that today we call originality. (He would likely have named it "invention.") But if "not imitated" as a meaning for the word *original* was at best emerging in Milton's time, it is unlikely that he would have understood the connection, so important to Bloom's theory, between the distinctiveness of a writing style and actual temporal priority. It is in the connection of these two senses of the term *original* that Bloom's theory is historically bounded, and this in turn is one reason Bloom has such difficulty accounting for Milton's canonical ambitions and achievement.

Another reason for Bloom's difficulty in accounting for Milton is that, in keeping with his definition of *original* as "initial, first, earliest," he figures an origin as a strictly unitary phenomenon. In contrast with earlier critics, who assumed that a poem consists of a variety of strands from previous literature—an image from here, some lines from there, an evocative phrase from someplace else—and thus has a multiplicity of origins, Bloom, who does not concern himself with these sorts of influences, conceives of an origin as profoundly singular. The agon between poets that is the most distinctive feature of Bloom's theory of poetry results from the fact that, again, "the commodity in which poets deal, their authority, their property, turns upon priority"; that priority or originality is conceived as a space that can be occupied by only one author at a time, prompting later poets to attempt a sort of king-of-the-hill (or, more precisely, Oedipal) struggle to oust their precursors from the privileged position of the origin and thus to usurp the authority which, in Bloom's view, is indivisible from anteriority (*Anxiety* 9). By contrast, Milton conceives of origins as binary in nature.

Bloom on Johnson on Milton

To see the impact of Bloom's view of origins on his understanding of the poetic tradition, consider his most extended examination of Milton: the analysis he offers in the chapter of *A Map of Misreading* titled "Milton and His Precursors." What follows is an extended reading of this chapter, in which I will argue that Bloom's treatment of Milton is not so much a straightforward account of Milton's place in the epic tradition as it is a Bloomian agon (with Johnson; critics contend in the same way as poets) for the authority that comes with priority.

In the chapter, Bloom claims that Milton achieves what all poets seek to achieve: he reverses time by writing in such a way as to make his precursors seem to be his imitators. In Bloom's eso-teric terms, this is *apophrades,* the sixth and ultimate revision-ary ratio, "the uncanny effect [of which] is that the new poem's achievement makes it seem to us...as though the later poet him-self had written the precursor's characteristic work" (*Anxiety* 16). Milton's capacity to effect an *apophrades* on his precursors, to come out a winner in the struggle for priority in which all strong poets engage, results from his particular manner of alluding to other authors: what Bloom terms a transumptive or metaleptic mode of allusion.

In Bloom's view, Milton developed this mode of allusion as a defense against Spenser, whom he acknowledged to Dryden was his "Original" (as Dryden reports it in the preface to *Fables Ancient and Modern*). Before examining this special mode of allusion, Bloom reiterates one of the central premises of his book—namely, that all original poetry results from a misread-ing of one's precursors—by drawing attention to a mistake that Milton makes about *The Faerie Queene* in his comments on Spenser in *Areopagitica:* Milton speaks of Spenser bringing Guyon into the cave of Mammon accompanied by the palmer, when in fact Guyon enters the cave of Mammon unaccompanied. "Milton's is no ordinary error," Bloom claims, "no mere lapse in memory, but is itself a powerful misinterpretation of Spenser and a strong defense against him" (*Map* 128). In Bloom's view, Milton had to make such a mistake about Guyon, had to believe that Spenser's hero was accompanied in his moment of temptation, in order to believe that his own presentation of Adam and Eve facing temptation unaccompanied by a spiritual superior represented an advance over the work of his precursor.

Having in this way evidenced his claim that all strong poetry arises from a misreading of one's precursors, Bloom begins to describe Milton's supremely effective mode of misreading, his "transumptive allusion," by invoking Samuel Johnson as the best authority on Milton's relation to his precursors. This citation of

Johnson, though, does more than just corroborate Bloom's point; it becomes the territory on which Bloom stages an agon with Johnson. Consider Bloom's quotation of Johnson, noting especially the ellipsis between the paragraphs and the phrase "adventitious image":

> Whatever be his subject, [Milton] never fails to fill the imagination. But his images and descriptions of the scenes or operations of Nature do not seem to be always copied from original form, nor to have the freshness, raciness, and energy of immediate observation. He saw nature, as Dryden expresses it, *through the spectacles of books*; and on most occasions calls learning to his assistance....
>
> ...But he does not confine himself within the limits of rigorous comparison: his great excellence is amplitude, and he expands the adventitious image beyond the dimensions which the occasion required. Thus, comparing the shield of Satan to the orb of the Moon, he crowds the imagination with the discovery of the telescope and all the wonders which the telescope discovers.[25]

Bloom then reproduces the passage from *Paradise Lost* to which Johnson refers in the second half of this quotation:

> He scarce had ceas't when the superiour Fiend
> Was moving toward the shoar; his ponderous shield
> Ethereal temper, massy, large and round,
> Behind him cast; the broad circumference
> Hung on his shoulders like the Moon, whose Orb
> Through Optic Glass the *Tuscan* Artist views
> At Ev'ning from the top of *Fesole*,
> Or in *Valdarno*, to descry new Lands,
> Rivers or Mountains in her spotty Globe.   (*PL* 1.283–91)

In comparing Satan's shield to the moon, Bloom observes, Milton alludes to Homer, who describes Achilles's shield as being like the moon, and to Spenser, who describes Radigund's shield as resembling the moon.[26] But, Bloom points out, Milton does not depict the same moon that his precursors depict: "Homer and Spenser emphasize the moonlike brightness and shining of the shields of Achilles and Radigund; Milton emphasizes size, shape, weight as the common feature of Satan's shield and the moon, for Milton's post-Galilean moon is more of a world and less of a light" (*Map* 133). Bloom, referring to Johnson's commentary on the Miltonic passage, calls Galileo's "Optic Glass" an "adventitious image," unnecessary to the picture that Milton is trying to paint. But while the image of the telescope may be adventitious with regard to the pictorial representation of Satan's shield, Bloom thinks it in another respect crucial, for it gives Milton a form of priority, the "priority of *interpretation*," over his precursors. That is to say, even though "Milton and Galileo are *late* . . . they see more, and more significantly, than Homer and Spenser, who were *early*" (*Map* 132–33). In this way, Milton turns "his tradition's priority over him into a lateness"; because of the seemingly adventitious image of the telescope, the moons described by Homer and Spenser come to seem like puerile imitations of a Miltonic original (*Map* 131).

The reading of Milton which I have just summarized is, in Bloom's own terms, a misreading—a misreading, however, not primarily of Milton, but of Johnson (whom Bloom calls "the greatest critic in the language" and "the first great diagnostician of the malady of poetic influence") (*Anxiety* 28). Bloom makes precisely the same sort of strategic error about Johnson that he showed Milton making about Spenser. His misreading of Johnson centers on the phrase "adventitious image." For Bloom, the adventitious image in Milton's description of Satan is the telescope; this is evident from Bloom's query, "why is Johnson's 'adventitious image,' Galileo and the telescope, present at all?" (*Map* 131–32).

Johnson, by contrast, uses the phrase "adventitious image" for what we now, following I. A. Richards, term the vehicle of a metaphor. This becomes more clear when we examine the whole of Johnson's text, of which Bloom's citation had reproduced only a part (his excision is indicated here by brackets):

Whatever be his subject, Milton never fails to fill the imagination. But his images and descriptions of the scenes or operations
of Nature do not seem to be always copied from original form,
nor to have the freshness, raciness, and energy of immediate
observation. He saw nature, as Dryden expresses it, *through the
spectacles of books;* and on most occasions calls learning to his
assistance. [The garden of Eden brings to his mind the vale of
Enna, where Proserpine was gathering flowers. Satan makes his
way through fighting elements, like *Argo* between the *Cyanean*
rocks, or *Ulysses* between the two *Sicilian* whirlpools, when he
shunned *Charybdis* on the *larboard.* The mythological allusions
have been justly censured, as not being always used with notice
of their vanity; but they contribute variety to the narration, and
produce an alternate exercise of the memory and the fancy.

His similes are less numerous, and more various, than those
of his predecessors.] But he does not confine himself within the
limits of rigorous comparison: his great excellence is amplitude, and he expands the adventitious image beyond the dimensions which the occasion required. Thus, comparing the shield
of Satan to the orb of the Moon, he crowds the imagination
with the discovery of the telescope and all the wonders which
the telescope discovers.[27]

Bloom's elliptical citation of Johnson, by effacing the context in
which the remark about the "adventitious image" occurs, significantly misrepresents Johnson's point; the excision makes it
seem — is designed to make it seem — as though Johnson is talking
about Milton's allusions throughout the quoted passage, when he
is in fact discussing first Milton's allusions and then his similes.

The paragraphs reproduced above represent just two in a series
of rapid-fire critical observations about various discrete aspects of
the epic: its divine machinery, episodes, integrity of design, moral
sentiments, and so on. The first paragraph discusses Milton's
highly erudite and allusive style; the second takes up an entirely
different aspect of the poem: similes. What Johnson wants to demonstrate in this second paragraph is the manner in which what we
now (following I. A. Richards) call the vehicle of Milton's similes
is often so fully elaborated in its own right that many of its details

have no correspondence with the tenor. To convey this insight, he coins the phrase "adventitious image" for what we today call a vehicle, he uses the term *occasion* for what we would call the tenor, and he chooses the word *crowding* for details in the vehicle that have no corresponding elements in the tenor. Miltonic similes are characterized by the fact that the adventitious image is developed so extensively that we cannot determine a point-by-point resemblance between it and its occasion. In this particular instance, Satan's shield is the occasion, the moon is the adventitious image, and the telescope is the expansion or crowding of that adventitious image.

Bloom's labeling the telescope, rather than the moon, as the "adventitious image" is no ordinary error, no mere lapse of attention while reading Johnson's text, but is itself a powerful misinterpretation of Johnson. Bloom's strategic excision makes it seem as though Johnson brings up the example of Satan's shield in the context of a discussion of Milton's allusions and thus that Johnson is adumbrating Bloom's argument concerning how Milton transumes his precursors. Why should Bloom arrange to make it appear that Johnson is anticipating his own notion of transumptive allusion? By making Johnson sound as though he is advancing Bloomian arguments, Bloom *effects* the very thing that he is ostensibly *describing* Milton as having effected: an *apophrades* of his precursor. Bloom is acting as he says poets act. And for a critic who will abide no distinction between criticism and poetry, it is not entirely surprising that a purported reading of Milton in fact turns out to be his own struggle to achieve priority over a critical predecessor.[28]

But if Bloom's chapter on Milton is in fact fairly characterized as a contest with Johnson for anteriority, what does that imply about its value as an account of Milton's place in the poetic tradition?[29] Does Milton here merely serve as Bloom's own "adventitious image," extrinsic to his genuine concern in this chapter (an agon with Johnson)? Or does Bloom manage simultaneously an *apophrades* of Johnson and a viable reading of Milton's poetic practice? We need, after all, look no further than *Paradise Lost* for an example of a work that aspires to be at once a poem and a kind of argument, justifying the ways of God to men. Or perhaps the better parallel would be the *Essay on Criticism*, in which Pope simultaneously enumerates and exemplifies a number of poetic and critical principles.

To gauge the explanatory force, as distinct from the poetic force, of Bloom's text, we might begin by noting that what Johnson is describing in the paragraph on Satan's shield is what has since come to be known as an epic or extended or "long-tailed" simile: a comparison in which the vehicle (or in Johnson's terminology, the "adventitious image") contains details that have no correspondence to the tenor (Johnson's "occasion"). Such "long-tailed" similes, as Nicolas Boileau points out in the sixth of his "Critical Reflections on Longinus," are especially characteristic of Homer.[30] And Milton, when constructing his own extended similes, follows Homer's practice rather than that of Virgil, in whose similes the details in the vehicle usually correspond, though often subtly, with elements of the tenor.[31] In any other critic than Bloom, we would regard as a mistake the inability to see that Johnson is discussing what is now known as an epic simile. Indeed, even in a theory that admits a large scope to the creative possibilities of misreading, the oversight is damaging. For if, as Bloom's argument would have it, Milton triumphs over his precursors through the technique of crowding his similes with "adventitious" contemporary details, then for the technique of the adventitious image itself to be borrowed from Homer would seem to represent a significant attenuation of Milton's supposed triumph. To describe the effect of Milton's allusions, as Bloom does on the basis of this reading, as being "to reverse literary tradition" may not be the best way to characterize Milton's relation to his precursors.

Originality and the Epic Tradition

If it is Bloom's conception of origins as unitary that motivates his agon with Johnson, and if his distortions of Johnson's argument resulting from that agon weaken Bloom's account of

Milton's position in the epic tradition, then perhaps a different understanding of origins might yield a more nuanced account of Milton's interpoetic relationships. As we have seen, the word *original* bears several distinct, even divergent, senses. The word has as its basic meaning "initial, first, earliest." To that sense is often added a notion of causality: "that from which something arises, proceeds, or is derived." In the substantive, an original is the pattern by which copies are made. Finally, in aesthetic parlance, *original* means "not derivative or dependent," or more precisely, "made, composed, or done by the person himself (not imitated from another)."

As I proposed earlier, one of the most common ways of graphically representing an origin—an image in which at least three of the senses of the word *origin* (primacy, causality, and discontinuity) combine—is what in Euclidian geometry is termed a ray: a line segment beginning at a point and extending indefinitely thence in one direction. The sense of primacy is captured in the point (actually referred to by mathematicians as the ray's *origin*); the line segment may depict a chain of consequences extending from that origin; and the blank space preceding the point represents the discontinuity from the past that makes the origin "not derivative or dependent." The conceptions of origins examined thus far can be coordinated with this threefold paradigm of origins contained in the image of the ray. Bloom's theory, for instance, focuses on the beginning point of the ray, stressing the unitary aspect of an origin, while the conventional modern understanding of originality focuses on the radical discontinuity between that point and the blank space that precedes it.[32]

The image of a ray also allows us to appreciate how the sense of the word *original* which came into the language toward the end of the seventeenth century, the sense of "not imitated from another," involves more than just a novel nuance accruing to an existing term, but represents instead an absolute reversal in the temporal perspective from which an origin is viewed. This newer understanding defines an origin primarily in relation to what comes before it, whereas the older sense of "that from which something arises, proceeds, or is derived" defines an origin in relation to what comes after it.

Milton, straddling the period in which the emphasis was gradually shifting from one of these definitions to the other, figures origins as binary in nature: an event, the poem insists, is only an origin in conjunction with that which follows from it and repeats it.[33] Just as in Euclidian geometry a line is determined by two points, the origin and one other point along its length, so too, in Milton's vision, are the consequences that follow from a particular event essential to determining the trajectory that the remaining consequences will follow, indeed essential even to that earlier event's *being* an origin.

I submit that to adopt Milton's unusual understanding of originality (an understanding of the concept that is likely the result of his writing during a historical period in which the meaning of the word *original* was in the process of changing) may provide us with a more satisfactory way than Bloom's of situating Milton within the epic tradition. Bloom would have it that Milton stands in an agonistic relation to his precursors, battling to occupy the king-of-the-hill position of origin, and indeed successfully outflanking his predecessors in this fashion. Such a picture, though, neglects the way in which Milton stations himself, in the construction of his similes, as an immediate follower of Homer.

A different and more comprehensive picture of Milton's place in the tradition of heroic poetry might be developed by adopting the same binary conception of origins evident within Milton's epic: a conception of an origin not as a single point, but as something that may be, and even must be, "completed." With such an idea in mind, we might describe Milton's place in the epic tradition by saying that Milton completes Homer differently than Virgil had. Such a formulation would square with Milton's own most explicit characterization of the position he wanted *Paradise Lost* to take up within the epic tradition. The proem to book 9 of *Paradise Lost* suggests that the epic tradition had followed a trajectory established by Virgil's imitation of Homer's martial episodes:

> the wrauth
> Of stern *Achilles* on his Foe pursu'd
> Thrice Fugitive about Troy Wall; or rage
> Of *Turnus* for *Lavinia* disespous'd,
> Or *Neptun's* ire or *Juno's*, that so long
> Perplex'd the *Greek* and *Cytherea's* Son.   (9.14–19)

It is customary to read this passage as Milton's rejection of the martial themes that had characterized classical epic. But there is another aspect of the epic tradition that he may be rejecting in these lines as well. By calling attention, through immediate juxtaposition, to the way in which Virgil's epic is built up by imitating the narrative sequences of Homer's epics (raging warriors contending around a fortification, resilient mariners overcoming divinely imposed obstacles in their wanderings), Milton may be suggesting that his new epic must imitate Homer at some level other than that at which Virgil had imitated him, namely, the level of narrative events. Apart from book 6 (which has the effect of demonstrating that he could have written a martial epic if he had wanted to), Milton largely chooses not to affiliate generically through the imitation of martial plot sequences. He suggests that, in establishing his generic affiliation, he must avoid Virgil's mode of imitating Homer. Instead, he imitates poetic features other than plot sequences, features that do not commit him to the martial ideology of pagan epic, including extended similes.

In his extended similes, Milton stations himself as an immediate descendant of Homer by including, as Homer was famous for doing, noncorresponding, "adventitious" details. In Homer, the vehicles of the extended similes frequently take readers off the battlefield, reminding them of the nonmilitary world outside the immediate conflict at Troy, the peacetime world of shepherds and craftsmen; in Milton the vehicles often pertain to wandering, exploring, seeking. The Galileo reference is typical in this regard; the Tuscan artist gradually descrying new geographical features on the moon exemplifies "patience" and, in defying church authority to defend his beliefs, the "heroic martyrdom" (literally witnessing) that Milton wants to make a new subject for epic poetry. Milton has always been regarded as at once a deeply traditional and a profoundly original artist. One way of reconciling this paradoxical mix of qualities, a way responsive to the developing understanding of originality in his day, would be to say that, where Virgil's imitative technique had established one trajectory for the heroic poem, Milton *completes Homer's originality differently,* steering the epic tradition toward fresh woods and pastures new.

In his treatment of *Paradise Lost,* David Quint characterizes Milton's relation to his poetic precursors in essentially Bloomian terms; Milton's "return to origins, to the ab-original events that even precede the biblical account of Creation, reverses the relationship between *Paradise Lost* and the tradition of earlier texts which it imitates. Those texts are now paradoxically recognized to be Milton's successors, to be secondary imitations of the archetypal story contained in his poem."[34] He contrasts Milton's understanding of tradition and individual talent with that expressed in a 1622 letter of Jean Chapelain, in which poetry in general was divinely founded, and all human authors, including even Homer, are possessed of at best the "less perfect," secondary originality involved in developing the various particular genres of poetry. In a view such as Chapelain's, where "all works in [the] tradition are...secondary, and none, not even Homer's can be set up as an absolute model, the competition between poets of the past and present can be conducted on a more equal footing. Originality is now only a relative quality of the poetic text and its value may fluctuate throughout literary history."[35] Quint associates this with the Romantic understanding of originality and characterizes Chapelain, at least tentatively, as more forward-looking than Milton, who "may be behind the prevailing taste of his own time...if Chapelain's letter is more representative."[36] But Milton's view allows a more thoroughgoing transumption by the later poet than just putting him on an "equal footing" with his precursor. In Milton's understanding, the later poet's imitation completes, and thereby actually *confers originality on,* the earlier poet; the two are, and only together, co-originators. Only with Milton's strenuous reorientation can Homero-Virgilian epic—with its focus on wrath, rage, and ire—become the vehicle for a narrative in which "Heav'nly love shall outdoo Hellish hate" (3.297).

Post-Romantic "originality" can drift toward superficial uniqueness, toward mere idiosyncrasy. If Milton's conception of originality is less proto-Romantic than that of Chapelain, and less post-Romantic than that of Bloom, it also allows for a more profound, more consequential, reworking of the literary past than either the equal footing that Chapelain envisions as a latecomer's most significant achievement relative to his precursors, or the apparent temporal outflanking that Bloom does.

FIVE

"Above th'Aonian Mount"

The Longinian Sublime in *Paradise Lost*

Perhaps the primary discursive mechanism by which *Paradise Lost* came to be canonized was the term *sublime*. In the year of Milton's death, Boileau published his translation of Longinus's treatise *Peri Hupsous* along with his own *Art of Poetry*; together the two treatises are credited with initiating a critical vogue in France and England centered around sublimity. Milton's poem was conveniently available as an example of literary sublimity, and a good deal of the early commentary on the poem cited this quality. In the prefatory poem appended to the 1674 and later editions of *Paradise Lost*, Marvell describes Milton's verse and theme as "sublime" (CM 2.1.5). In his prefatory poem, Samuel Barrow similarly focuses on the transcendent nature of Milton's imagination: "Haec quicunque leget tantum cecinesse putabit / Maeonidem ranas, Virgilium culices" (who reads this will deem that Homer sang only of frogs, and Virgil of gnats) (CM 2.1.2).

Although he did not use the term *sublime* specifically, Dryden probably has sublimity in mind when he speaks of the "loftiness" for which Homer was known — but which Milton has surpassed, as he has surpassed Virgil in "majesty." Addison proposed that "Milton's chief talent, and indeed his distinguishing excellence, lies in the sublimity of his thoughts." Johnson asserted that "the characteristic quality of his poem is sublimity."[1]

Nonetheless, the standard critical view among historians of the sublime has been that Milton himself ironically never understood the critical concept as it would come to be formulated by Boileau and subsequent literary theorists and as it was to figure in the early reception and canonization of his epic. In his account of the sublime, Samuel Monk acknowledges that Milton knew Longinus. (A Greek and Latin edition of *Peri Hupsous* was available in England from 1636, and a translation, by Milton's republican colleague John Hall, from 1652. And Milton undoubtedly knew and valued Longinus, for in *Of Education* he recommends that students read him as they near the completion of their studies.) But Monk argues that Milton would seem "not to have felt Longinus' charm," as evidenced by the fact that he lists Longinus merely as one of the teachers of "a graceful and ornate rhetoric."[2] That is to say that although he is remarkable for mentioning Longinus, Milton evidently regarded *Peri Hupsous* merely as a rhetorical handbook like that of Quintilian or Cicero, and not (as the work came to be viewed by eighteenth century critics) as a theoretical treatise exploring a transcendent poetic quality. It is therefore, in Monk's view, to be accounted "a strange paradox that the most sublime of English poets should not have caught from Longinus the suggestion of the sublime as the expression of ultimate values in art, beyond the reach of rhetoric and her handmaidens, the rules."[3]

Annabel Patterson, however, challenges the traditional critical account, asserting, "Milton himself *intended* his poem to be seen as a demonstration of sublime themes and effects."[4] I believe Patterson is correct, and in this chapter I will substantiate her assertion by examining allusions in *Paradise Lost* that transcend their classical sources in a manner suggested by Longinus's treatise.

Longinus in *Of Education*

Let us begin by probing Monk's "strange paradox," considering in more detail Milton's reference to Longinus in *Of Education*. Given the paucity of critical reference to Longinus by European humanists before Boileau, as documented by Jules Brody, it is remarkable that Milton mentions him at all.[5] Nevertheless, as Monk suggests, merely listing Longinus as someone from whom students could learn "a graceful and ornate rhetoric" might not seem to suggest that Milton read *Peri Hupsous* as treating a sublime that represented "ultimate values in art, beyond the reach of rhetoric and her handmaidens, the rules." In Milton's day, the various terms by which Longinus's *hupsous* might have been translated (*height, loftiness,* or even *sublimity*) would generally have been linked to the elevated *diction* stipulated by the principle of decorum as appropriate for the most serious poetic topics, rather than to the transcendental *experiences* of art and nature with which sublimity would come to be associated through the late-seventeenth and eighteenth century developments of the critical concept.

As Brody points out, "those who knew *Peri Hupsous* at all habitually called it not *De Sublimitate* but *De sublimi genere dicendi, De grandi genere orationis* [or] *De sublimi oratione.* As they saw it Longinus's book dealt with the *genus grande,* the most elaborate of the three *genera dicendi* into which ancient rhetoric usually divided discourse," and again "he was invoked most often in the company of Aristotle, Cicero, Demetrius, and Quintilian, as a theoretician of the grand style, a teacher of composition, an authority on points of philology."[6] In appropriations of *Peri Hupsous* before Boileau, in other words, Longinus would have been read as providing instruction on how to write in the highest of the three stylistic registers—"lofty, mean or low"—that the principle of decorum suggested were appropriate for various poetic subjects. Langbaine's 1636 facing-page Latin translation, for instance, immediately translates Longinus's simple *peri hypsous* (of high things) as "de Sublimi genere Oratatonis." Hall's translation rendered the title as "Of the Height of Eloquence," and his dedication to Bullstrode Whitelock indicates clearly that he regarded the treatise as a rhetorical handbook. Indeed, Hall seems to regard the treatise as pertaining not just to rhetoric but to oratory specifically; he regards it as being potentially "obsolete, and to this age not at all pertinent" because commonwealths have become too large for their leaders to address the entire populace at once: "in civil matters we are to speak to the few and not the many."[7] It was Boileau's specific theoretical innovation, according to Brody, to treat *Peri Hupsous* "less [as] a manual of rhetoric than an essay in esthetics" (88).

One aspect of Milton's handling of Longinus in *Of Education* hints, however, that, at least on some level he may have understood the sublime as more than just one of the three levels of diction, but as representing something more like the fundamental aesthetic principle it was to become for critics following Boileau. For immediately after he mentions Longinus, Milton's otherwise carefully plotted educational system is disrupted. In his proposed educational program, Milton says that after logic would come rhetoric, including Longinus, "to which poetry would be made subsequent, or indeed rather precedent" (CM 4.286). Milton suddenly seems unsure whether the study of poetry and poetics should precede or follow the study of rhetoric.

Perhaps the mention of Longinus caused this disruption, for his treatise straddles the boundary between rhetoric and poetics. Its advice is directed both to orators and to poets; its examples drawn from Homer as often as Demosthenes. That is to say, Longinus's treatise not only teaches "those organic arts which inable men to discourse and write perspicuously, elegantly, and according to the fitted stile of lofty, mean or lowly," but he is also one of the teachers of "that sublime Art which in *Aristotles*

Poetics, in *Horace* and the *Italian* Commentaries of *Castelvetro, Tasso, Mazzoni,* and others, teaches what the laws are of a true *Epic* poem, what of a *Dramatic,* what of a *Lyric"* (CM 4.286). Longinus's name falling precisely at the pivot point in Milton's treatise between rhetoric and poetics represents an anticipation of the theoretical innovation with which Boileau is credited, that of treating *Peri Hupsous* as an aesthetic treatise rather than merely a rhetorical handbook. Moreover, at least two of the qualities of poetry that provide the grounds for Milton's wavering on whether to teach poetry before rhetoric—that poetry is more "passionate" and more "simple"—may also have been partly suggested by Longinus. Through much of his treatise, he mentions *pathos* (the Greek word for powerful emotion that is the root of the English *passion*) in the same breath with *hupsos.* And, as Boileau would come (following Longinus) to formulate the concept, "simplicity is not merely a characteristic of the sublime; it is its essence."[8]

"With No Middle Flight"

Apart from his handling of Longinus in *Of Education,* an even more significant sign that Milton was deliberately striving after sublimity—as Longinus had formulated the notion and as critics after Boileau would come to understand it—is that his *manner* of alluding to passages in Homer (and other authors) seems to have been suggested to him by Longinus's emphasis on rivalry between sublime authors. Longinus mentions poetic imitation as one of the means toward the sublime: "there is another road, besides those we have mentioned, which leads to sublimity. What and what manner of road is this? Zealous imitation of the great prose writers and poets of the past" (*Sublime* 211). Moreover, he discusses the creative afflatus that results when we experience another author's sublimity: "the true sublime naturally elevates us: uplifted with a sense of proud exaltation, we are filled with joy and pride, as if we had ourselves produced the very thing we heard" (179). Furthermore, in a consideration of

Plato's appropriations of Homeric phrases, Longinus connects the sublime to authorial rivalry, admiring how Plato strove "with heart and soul, to contest the prize with Homer, like a young antagonist with one who had already won his spurs" (213). Such passages may have suggested to Milton one of the main uses he makes of his epic predecessors: subtly altering their phrasing to conjure a cosmos infinitely more vast than their own.

Here again we must be careful because, even apart from Longinus, the Renaissance theory of poetic imitation, "aemulatio," stressed that it should involve competitive rivalry, and not mere borrowing or servile imitation. Using the apian metaphor common for expressing the concept, Petrarch said, "the bees would enjoy no glory if they did not transform those things they found into something else which was better."[9] Quintilian had counseled, "Even those who do not seek the heights should contend rather than follow. For he who tries to be in front may equal even if he cannot surpass. No one, however, can equal the person whose footsteps he thinks he must tread in: for the follower will always of necessity be behind."[10] Erasmus said, "The true imitator tries not so much to say identical things as similar things, sometimes not even similar things but equivalent things. The challenger endeavours to speak even better if he can."[11] Milton himself articulates the principle when, in *Eikonoklastes*, he chastises the king for borrowing one of David's psalms: "For such kind of borrowing as this, *if it be not better'd by the borrower*, among good Authors is accounted Plagiarie" (CM 5.259; emphasis mine).

But where a kind of one-upmanship was expected in interpoetic relations by the compositional theory of his day, Milton does not simply top his classical sources; he surpasses them by an order of magnitude, in a manner suggesting that he did indeed in some measure understand Longinus along the lines of Boileau and his followers. In many of Milton's allusions, the passage he echoes serves as a point of departure from which he can discernibly surpass his predecessors' poetic achievement. When the battling angels begin tearing up hills to throw at one another, Raphael says, "and now all Heav'n / Had gon to wrack, with ruin over-spred" had the Almighty Father not intervened, sending the Son to end the conflict (6.669–70). Milton's phrasing here is modeled on a passage from book 8 of the *Iliad*. Diomedes has just killed Hector's charioteer, and the narrator tells us, "And now there would have been fighting beyond control, and destruction. / Now they would have been driven and penned like sheep against Ilion, / Had not the father of gods and men sharply perceived them" (130–32). Milton has borrowed Homer's "and now...had not" syntax, and for a critic like Charles Martindale, that is all there is to this echo; he refers to this sort of allusion as a mere appro-priation of "epic articulation."[12] But, of course, we may also note the greater grandeur of Milton's description. Within the scope of the *Iliad*, the entire Trojan army being pinned against the walls of Troy would be a development of great magnitude. But beside all heaven going to wrack, it looks positively insignificant. When Milton has the warring angels in book 6 pluck "the seated Hills" by their "shaggy tops" and hurl them, "confusion heapt / Upon confusion," he recalls Homer's description of the Titans who "were minded to pile Ossa on Olympos, and above Ossa / Pelion of the trembling leaves." And this allusion surpasses Homer in a way similar to the "and now...had not" allusion.

The thought of Titans piling mountains on top of one another in order to battle against the gods is sublime. But Milton, in addition to capturing the *height* to which piled mountains would ascend, captures the *depth* of the pit that would be created by their dis-placement when he mentions that amid the flying mountains, "under ground" the contending angels "fought in dismal shade, / Infernal noise" (6.666–67). That mention of depth at least doubles the magnitude of Homer's conception. Similarly, when describ-ing Satan's "dilation" as he squares off against Gabriel, Milton says that he "stood / Like *Teneriff* or *Atlas* unremov'd: / His stat-ure reacht the Skie," a conception that is modeled on Homer's description of Strife, who "grows until she strides on the earth with her head striking heaven" (*PL* 4.986–87; *Iliad* 4.443); here, by comparing Satan to "*Teneriff* or *Atlas* unremov'd," Milton adds to the sublime *height* of Homer's Strife further sublime dimensions of bulk, stability, and fixity.

Other of Milton's allusions to Homer work in this same way, using Homer's sublime conceptions merely as a point of reference to be exponentially surpassed. Consider an allusion that, on the surface, might seem an almost mechanical instance of topping. In book 8 of the *Iliad*, Zeus prohibits the other Olympian gods from assisting the human warriors fighting at Troy. He threatens to throw anyone who disobeys into Tartarus, which he describes as being "as far beneath the house of Hades as from earth the sky lies" (16). Virgil doubles Homer's measure. As Aeneas is guided through the underworld by the Sibyl, she tells him that "Tartarus itself / then plunges downward, stretching *twice* as far / as is the view of heaven, high Olympus" (6.577; emphasis mine). When the Miltonic narrator is describing the place of torment that God has prepared for the rebellious angels, he says that it is "As far remov'd from God and light of Heav'n / As from the Center thrice to th'utmost Pole" (1.73–74). Milton picks up the "as far as" syntax of the Homeric and Virgilian phrases, and his "thrice" might initially seem to take Virgil's topping of Homer ("twice") and go it one better. But, given Milton's unit of measure (center to pole), the "thrice" actually does more than expand the Virgilian image by 50 percent. By using the description of distance that he does, Milton insists that the underworld is not inside the center of the earth, as was imagined by pagan (and even many Christian) writers, but rather in some some entirely separate region of the cosmos. For, even if this "Pole" is only the terrestial pole (and not, as is likely, the celestial pole), a distance three times the radius of the earth cannot be contained within the earth itself. Milton renders woefully insignificant the very scale of measurement by which Homer and Virgil obtain their impressive images of something being as far, or twice as far, below ground as a mountain rises above ground. Indeed, this way of conveying sublime distances may have been not just generally, but very specifically, suggested to Milton by Longinus, who, in treating a passage on how Hera's horses leap across the horizon at a stride, marvels, "So supreme is the grandeur of this, one might well say that if the horses of heaven take two consecutive strides there will then be no place found for them in the world" (*Sublime* 187).

The description 20 lines earlier of the rebellious angels "rolling in the fiery Gulf" works in much the same way. Milton says that the "horrid crew / Lay vanquisht" for "Nine times the Space that measures Day and Night." The choice of a nine-day period here is probably influenced by Homeric epic. In Homer (and Hesiod) the compound noun ἐννῆμαρ, nine days, is used formulaically. In what might serve as the closest parallel for the Miltonic passage, for instance, Odysseus floats for nine days on the ocean after his ship is wrecked and before reaching Calypso's island of Ogygia (*Odyssey* 12.447). We might also recall that in Hesiod's theomachia, the Titans fall for nine days when thrown down from Olympus by Zeus.[13] But Milton's phrasing, "Nine times the Space that measures Day and Night," does more than just draw ἐννῆμαρ out through circumlocution from a word into a lingering full verse. By introducing the reference to space, it also suggests the immense expanse of *territory* that the bodies of the fallen angels cover: nine sun-spans worth.

For another example of such allusions, where subtle elements of Milton's adaptation place his descriptions on an entirely different order of magnitude than those of his source, consider the description of Beelzebub. Satan says of him that, "Cloth'd with transcendent brightness [he] didst out-shine / Myriads though bright" (*PL* 1.86–87). Again the phrasing is modeled on a passage from Homer. Nausikaa frolicking with her handmaidens is compared by the Homeric narrator to Artemis among her nymphs: "And above them all, she held her head and her face, / Easily the most conspicuous, though they all were lovely" (*Odyssey* 6.107–08; my translation). Roughly the same idea is conveyed by the Miltonic and Homeric verses: that one being surpasses a group of others by which he or she is surrounded. And Milton's repetition of "brightness...bright" is probably modeled on Homer's repetition of "all...all" (πασάων...πᾶσαι). But Beelzebub's transcendence is of an entirely higher order than that of Artemis because of the quality that is compared in each case. To be more beautiful than a group of nymphs means that Artemis is more beautiful than *any* of her companions, but since luminescence can aggregate, to be brighter than a myriad of bright beings is to outshine the *sum total* of their brightness; Beelzebub is brighter than *all* of his companions combined.

Just as the cosmological scale of Milton's universe dwarfs that of Homer and Virgil, so too does its historical scale. When Milton begins the catalog of devils, he asks his muse to "Say...thir Names, then known, who first, who last / Rous'd from the slumber on that fiery Couch" (*PL* 1.376–77). The phrasing is modeled on a moment in book 5 of the *Iliad*, when Homer asks, "Who was the first, who the last" Greek soldier that Hector killed (703). But the insertion of "then known" introduces a historical perspective that surpasses anything imagined by Homer, or even the extended historical timeframe of Virgil's epic. Three widely separated temporal moments are evoked by the phrase. In the present moment of Milton's narrative, these beings do not have names. Centuries further on they will have names, the names of false gods who tempt the Israelites "to forsake / God their creator" (*PL* 1.368–69). In the moment from which Milton is writing, millennia further on still, when these false gods have been discredited (and silenced) by the true God, they are only names. Within the temporal framework of Milton's epic, which in effect takes in all time, even the millennium-long growth of the Roman Empire from its founding by Aeneas to its moment of glory under Augustus represents a relatively insignificant time-span.

Milton, in short, uses Homeric and Virgilian passages to establish a standard of sublimity which his own adaptations then thoroughly eclipse. Pagan antiquity, as Milton thus presents it, was not only religiously misguided; it was imaginatively stunted as well. When listing the Greek gods within his catalog of devils, he says of them, "on the Snowy top / Of cold *Olympus* [they] rul'd the middle Air / Thir highest Heav'n" (*PL* 1.515–17). This reference to the "middle Air" as the highest point to which the pagan imagination could reach when imagining its deities may provide the specific referent for Milton's claim that his own epic will "with no middle flight…soar / Above th'Aonian mount" into heavenly realms of a magnitude inconceivable to pagan authors (1.14–15).

Longinus in the Mid-Seventeenth Century

Perhaps the most striking evidence that Milton, as Patterson puts it, "*intended* his poem to be seen as a demonstration of sublime themes and effects," is that, of the seven Homeric passages Longinus adduces to exemplify sublimity of thought and of emotion, *Paradise Lost* alludes to three of them and has passages closely related to two others. As an example of the principle that some passages can be sublime even without emotion, Longinus instances Homer's description of the Titans who "were minded to pile Ossa on Olympos, and above Ossa / Pelion of the trembling leaves," which Milton recalls during the war in heaven when the angels pluck "the seated Hills" by their "shaggy tops" and hurl them, "confusion heapt / Upon confusion" (*Odyssey* 11.315–16; *PL* 6.644–45, 668–69). Similarly, Homer's Strife, who "grows until she strides on the earth with her head striking heaven," for Longinus measures the loftiness of Homer's imagination as much as of Strife itself (*Iliad* 4.443; *Sublime* 185). At the end of book 4, as he squares off against Gabriel, the narrator says of Satan that "His stature reacht the Skie" (986–88).

Longinus finds the stride of Hera's horses to be sublime: "As far as into the hazing distance a man can see with / his eyes, who sits in his eyrie gazing on the wine-blue water, / as far as this is the stride of the god's proud neighing horses" (*Iliad* 5.770–72). Milton's description of the archangels' travel as they bear God's errands "over moist and dry / O're Sea and Land" is modeled on a later description of Hera's horses (*PL* 3.652–53; *Iliad* 14.307). Longinus cites the sublimity of Poseidon's potential to "break the earth open" that "the houses of the dead lie open to men and immortals," a sublimity Milton tries to recapture when he asserts of the angels' battle that "now all Heav'n / Had gon to wrack, with ruin overspred" (*Iliad* 20.63–64; *PL* 6.669–70). Longinus finds it sublime that Ajax begs Zeus for daylight, even if he should die: "in shining daylight destroy us, if to destroy us be now your pleasure" (*Iliad* 17.646–47). Milton does not imitate this particular passage, but Moloch's lack of concern lest God's "utmost ire...quite consume us and reduce / To nothing this essential" is modeled on another death-defying speech of Ajax (*PL* 2.95–97; *Iliad* 15.509–13). In writing *Paradise Lost*, in other words, Milton seems to have been intent on recalling most of the Homeric passages that Longinus had singled out as examples of the sublime, and then surpassing even them in sublimity.

There is another set of facts, moreover, that suggests that the Longinian sublimity of *Paradise Lost* is the result of a deliberate design on the part of Milton, intuiting the imminent prominence of Longinus on the critical scene. The people who knew Milton directly, and would therefore likely have been privy to his guiding poetic standards and ambitions, use the word *sublime* to characterize his work. Andrew Marvell ends his encomiastic poem with the claim that "Thy Verse created like thy Theme sublime, / In Number, Weight and Measure, needs not Rhime" (CM 2.1.5). Milton's nephew, Edward Phillips (who had been educated under a program like the one sketched in *Of Education*), hammers home the concept when he claims that *Paradise Lost* will be recognized as a heroic poem that has "achieved perfection in this kind of poetry," whether readers "regard the sublimity of the subject, or the combined pleasantness and majesty of the style, or the majesty of the invention, or the supremely natural images and descriptions."[14]

Finally, early readers seem to have responded, at least on some level, to the sublime poetic rivalry manifested by Milton's epic.

An appreciation of this effect seems implicit, for instance, in Barrow's claim that "who reads this will deem that Homer sang only of frogs, and Virgil of gnats" as well as in the report of Sir Fleetwood Sheppard of Dryden's response to his first reading of Milton's epic: "This Man...Cuts us All Out, and the Ancients too."[15] Milton seems in some degree, then, to have anticipated the development in critical theory and terminology by which his epic would come to be canonized. As in the case of *originality*, what alerted Milton to the imminent emergence of *sublimity* as a key critical term—and what I call a "discursive mechanism of canonization"—may have been his attention to the canonical status of Homer in the seventeenth century. Boileau himself would go on to be engaged in the most overt and direct canonical struggle of the age, the *querelle des anciens et des modernes*, and as Brody points out, his championing of Homer in the *querelle* was of a piece with his interest in the sublime.[16] But even earlier, in the years in which Milton planned, composed, and published *Paradise Lost*, the canonical status of Homer was increasingly coming to be produced in connection with the Longinian sublime. As one index of the development, consider that, while the notes in Chapman's 1611 translation of the *Iliad* do not mention Longinus, the notes of the next major English translation, that of John Ogilby in 1660, pointedly do. In connection with Ajax's desire for the sun to rise so that should he die, he would at least be seen dying heroically, Ogilby's note reads, "a Passion (saith Diogenes Longinus, admiring it as an Heroick pitch) well becoming Ajax, he begging not life of Jupiter, but the sudden approach of light, he not doubting then to hew out himself a Sepulcher worthy of his own valor, and that though Jove himselfe should combate with him" (390).[17]

Kirsti Simonsuuri connects Homer's mid-seventeenth century canonical fortunes with the emerging interest in the sublime. In tracing the canonical status of Homer through the centuries, she characterizes the Middle Ages as beginning a period of "decline" and even the Renaissance as a period in which "there was a note of definite disappointment with Homer."[18] She dates a "renewal of interest in Homer" precisely to the later seventeenth century focus on Longinus and the sublime: "for the point about 'Longinus' is that he does give good reasons for rating Homer high as a poet and these served to counterbalance the more specific objections to him as a writer of epic" by Scaliger, Vida, and others. (The silence of *Peri Hupsous* concerning Virgil may have been taken as an implicit preference for his Greek predecessor.) Although Simonsuuri regards the key turning point as Boileau's translation of Longinus, she argues, "from about 1640 onwards there was a stream of books on the Homeric background, lexica and critical commentaries, so that by the time Boileau produced his Longinus in 1674 there was a basis for a renewal of interest in Homer."[19]

Among the stream of books to which she alludes during the period from 1640 onward is James Duport's *Homeri gnomologia,* the preface to which lauds Homer in part for his "ineffable sublimity of style" (*ineffibilis styli sublimitas*).[20] The word *sublimis* had conventionally been attached to Homer throughout the Renaissance. For instance, the *Epitheta,* an enormously popular handbook of poetic epithets compiled by Jean Tixier de Ravise, lists *sublimis* as one of the possible epithets for Homer (but not for Virgil).[21] Again, the appearance of this epithet in Ravise comes well before the term *sublime* became freighted with the special associations it had in Longinus and his late-seventeenth and eighteenth century commentators. But Duport's *ineffibilis* suggests that this conventional term for Homer had by 1660 begun to acquire some of the force that it was to have for those commentators as a designation of poetic effects that defy full explanation by the rules of art.

In Meric Casaubon's 1654 *Treatise concerning Enthusiasm,* respect for Longinus, "not inferior to [Cicero] in point of judgment and reputation," goes hand in hand with the highest admiration for Homer, of whom "there is no commendation can be given unto man...but I should be more ready to adde to it, then to detract." Moreover, Casaubon repeatedly lauds Homer's poetry with a term, *ravishment*, that recalls Longinus's description of the effect of the sublime.[22]

Through the mid-seventeenth century, then, even before Boileau brought the Longinian sublime into intense focus for European literary critics, the canonical status of Homer's epics was increasingly produced in connection with a nascent understanding of, and value for, the quality of sublimity. Milton, among the earliest of English writers to express a regard for Longinus, seems to have written (and packaged) *Paradise Lost* with the hope that it, like Homer's epics, might be appreciated and canonized as a sublime poem. As Death "snuff[s] the smell / Of mortal change on Earth," Milton seems to have snuffed the smell of critical change in France and to have built, in *Paradise Lost*, a sort of bridge between an earlier conception of Longinian sublimity and the energetic late-seventeenth century reformulation of that concept. Monk's "strange paradox that the most sublime of English poets should not have caught from Longinus the suggestion of the sublime as the expression of ultimate values in art" is only a paradox if one goes looking for explicit aesthetic theorizing and regards the mention in *Of Education* (and not *Paradise Lost*) as Milton's last word on Longinian sublimity.

Six

"Instruct Me"

Institutional Considerations in Milton's Evolving Literary Ambitions

In 1642, in *The Reason of Church Government,* Milton introduces an extended digression in which he shares with his reader his literary ambitions. He indicates his desire to "leave something so written to aftertimes, as they should not willingly let it die" and offers a consideration of the genres in which he might compose that lasting work: whether "that epick form," or whether "Dramatick constitutions…shall be found more doctrinal and exemplary to a Nation," or whether "occasion shall lead" to compose "magnific Odes and Hymns" (CM 3.1:236–38). The contemporaneous Trinity Manuscript seems to suggest that in the early 1640s Milton was leaning toward the composition of tragedies, but by the late 1650s he had settled on epic as the genre in which he would make his bid for literary immortality. I propose that this change in Milton's generic focus can be explained in terms of his canonical ambitions—in terms, more specifically, of his reflections on the role of institutions in the preservation and dissemination of literary works.[1] "Aftertimes" for Milton, are not vaguely imagined future generations of readers, but involve specific institutions that might serve to perpetuate his great poems.

In his writings on the process of canon formation, John Guillory stresses that the composition of the literary canon is not simply the aggregate result of individual readers' evaluative judgments on various literary works; the literary canon can only be understood fully by considering the institutions responsible for the preservation and dissemination of literary texts: "An individual's judgment that a work is great does nothing in itself to preserve that work, unless that judgment is made in a certain institutional context, a setting in which it is possible to insure the *reproduction* of the work, its continual reintroduction to generations of readers."[2] Just as Milton seems to have composed *Paradise Lost* with an eye toward the terms of literary approbation operative (and emerging) in his day, so too did he reflect on the institutions responsible for the preservation and dissemination of literary texts and to which he might entrust his work for such perpetuation.

We can discern those reflections in his ongoing deliberations regarding the genre in which he should compose his great work or works. Milton seems intuitively to have understood the principle of canon formation Guillory describes: that, if his work were to survive, it would only be because some institution undertook to introduce it to successive generations of readers. What that institution should be was not immediately clear, and this ambiguity explains the uncertainty revealed in *The Reason of Church Government* regarding the genre in which he should compose. But over time Milton came to believe that academic institutions could be entrusted with the task of perpetuating a vernacular epic, and his generic indecision was resolved once he could imagine such institutions undertaking to perpetuate his literary work.

Since the late eighteenth century, Guillory demonstrates, the institution responsible for the reintroduction of literary works to successive generations of readers has been the school. But for Milton, the question of what institution could guarantee the survival of his great work was for a time an open one. Although he eventually did settle on the institution of the school as an appropriate site for the dissemination and perpetuation of his work, he had to discover, and could not simply assume, its appropriateness. *Paradise Lost* shows signs of having been composed with the institution of the school in mind, including similarities with the earliest textbooks. This chapter traces Milton's developing realization that academic institutions were the ones most likely to ensure the survival of his work.[3]

Epic, Tragedy, Ode

Critics generally derive the principle that accounts for Milton's generic vacillation from the passage in *The Reason of Church Government* in which he weighs the genres of epic, tragedy, and ode against one another. Milton, the usual explanation runs, eventually came to believe that epic was the genre most "doctrinal and exemplary to a nation" after believing for a while that tragedy might be. While I take seriously Milton's pedagogical ambitions, I suggest that the doctrinal superiority of one genre over another is not the central concern underlying the famous passage in which the virtues of epic, tragedy, and ode are compared. In the passage as a whole, Milton seems not so much concerned with the instructiveness of his projected work as with its mere survival. Preceding the passage on the genres is one in which Milton confesses that the *"vital* signes" in his early poems have prompted him to believe he might "leave something so written to aftertimes, as they should not willingly let it *die,"* and so he has begun to calculate how he might write "as men buy Leases, for three *lives* and downward" (CM 3:1.235–36; emphasis mine). To be sure, the "instruction of [his] country" occurs to him as being of fundamental importance in such an enterprise; Milton would not have wanted his works to live on as mere "verbal curiosities." But the emphasis falls on creating an enduring work of art. Milton seems still very much afflicted by "that last infirmity of noble mind."

Of course, there are several considerations that enter into Milton's generic deliberations. He evidently wants to write in one of the genres that ancient or modern critical authority had deemed the noblest of all. He also seems concerned that it be a literary type with both classical and biblical exemplars; epic is only to be considered if Job is as viable an example of the genre as the *Iliad*, and tragedy only if Revelation has the same claim to that title as the plays of Euripides and Sophocles. But it is only by adding to these criteria (critical preeminence and classical-biblical congruity) the criterion of an institutional site responsible for perpetuating his work that we can fully account for the generic options Milton presents himself and for the temporary inclination away from his early plans of writing an epic and toward composition in the tragic genre.

Institutional considerations serve, first of all, to explain the presence of ode in Milton's generic deliberations. If critical preeminence and classical-biblical congruity were his only criteria, Milton's schema would have taken the form of a choice between tragedy and epic. Tragedy had the authority of Aristotle for being the highest of all the genres, and epic the authority of many Italian theorists of the Renaissance. But no critical authority had argued that the ode had a claim to the highest place. Its inclusion, I would argue, is a result of the third criterion: Milton could envision an institution in which odes could be disseminated. If, as the passage seems to indicate, Milton imagined creating a kind of hymnbook, such a work could be received, disseminated, and perpetuated within the institution of the church.[4] By contrast, in the early 1640s Milton had difficulty determining what institution could similarly guarantee the survival of epic or tragedy.

The second aspect of Milton's deliberations that institutional considerations help to illuminate is his seeming preference in the early 1640s for tragedy. The Trinity Manuscript lists almost a hundred possible subjects for tragedy and only one subject for a heroic poem. This temporary favoring of tragedy, I would argue, results from the fact that Milton could at least envision the emergence of an institution appropriate for the dissemination of dramatic compositions. He describes his vision in *The Reason of Church Government,* opining immediately after the deliberations on genre that:

> it were happy for the Common wealth if our Magistrates, as in those famous governments of old, would take into their care...the managing of our publick sports and festival pastimes, that they might be...such as...civilize, adorn, and make discreet our minds by the learned and affable meeting of frequent Academies, and the procurement of wise and artfull recitations sweetened with eloquent and graceful inticements to the love and practice of justice, temperance, and fortitude...in Theaters, porches, or what other place, or way may win most upon the people to receiv at once both recreation, & instruction. (CM 3:1.239–40)

What Milton seems to have in mind is a state-sponsored theater that would commission morally edifying dramas.[5]

He may, in fact, have been imagining a state-sponsored theater such as the one in Athens for which Aeschylus, Sophocles, and Euripides composed. In the Trinity Manuscript, Milton seems to be working out the plots not only for individual tragedies, but also for tragic trilogies. On the first page of the manuscript devoted to plans for tragedy are three sketches for a drama involving the fall of Adam and Eve. Also on that page, under the heading "Other Tragedies," and between the first two *dramatis personae* for a tragedy on the Fall, are three titles: "Adam in Banishment," "The Flood," and "Abram in Aegypt." These three tragedies (or two of them in conjunction with *Paradise Lost*) might form a trilogy on individuals selected by God for providential care. On the next page—side by side instead of one atop the other, as the majority of entries are arranged—are the titles "The Deluge" and "Sodom," two other tragedies that might combine with *Paradise Lost,* in this case to form a trilogy on the catastrophic consequences of sin.

Immediately beneath these two titles are brief sketches for two tragedies, one on Dinah and one on Tamar. These two plays could also combine with the proposed *Paradise Lost* to form a trilogy, for all deal directly with marriage. Moreover, the action of the proposed "Thamar" develops as follows: "Juda is found to have bin the author of that crime wch he condemn'd in Tamar"; this might have been intended as a thematic counterpart for the way in which, in the proposed *Paradise Lost*, Adam and Eve "returne [and] accuse one another but especially Adam layes the blame to his wife."[6] After the tragedies on Dinah and Tamar, there follow sketches for three possible tragedies on Elijah: Elias in the mount, Elisaeus Hydrochoos, and Elisaeus Menutes Sive in Dothaimis.[7] The "festival pastimes" Milton urges Parliament to take into their care, then, might include events like Athens' Great Dionysia in which Aeschylus, Sophocles, and Euripides competed with their tragic trilogies.

What prevented Milton from envisioning an institution in which an epic could be received and preserved? I believe his trip to Italy had suggested to him that the political and institutional context appropriate for the production and reception of an epic poem was the context from which had emerged the one modern poem he deemed worthy of consideration alongside the epics of antiquity, namely, what Milton had seen when he visited Tasso's patron, Manso, in Italy: a powerful but learned nobleman who could serve as a patron and around whom were private academies, in which "every one must give some proof of his wit and reading" (CM 3.1:235). The early Commonwealth did not offer such a milieu, and Milton seems on some level to have recognized as much. In the passage from *The Reason of Church Government*, he remarks that Tasso gave "to a prince of Italy" a choice as to what subject he should treat, going on to assert that "it haply would be no rashnesse, from an equal diligence and inclination, to present the like offer in our own ancient stories" (CM 3.1:237). But to whom? The missing indirect object seems to reflect Milton's awareness that England is unlike Italy in that it does not offer compositional circumstances appropriate for the heroic poem.

Ironically, while he was visiting Italy, Milton lost his only substitute for the Italian academies: his friend, Charles Diodati. "Epitaphium Damonis" figures Diodati in terms that show Milton was thinking of him in conjunction with the private academies he had seen in Italy. Thyrsis and Damon are described as having "followed the same studies from youth." Diodati is said to be "for genius, for learning and for other splendid virtues, a youth outstanding."[8] Manso is mentioned in the poem. And in the argument, Milton notes that he and Diodati, figured in the poem as Thyrsis and Damon, were friends—"erant amici"—perhaps recalling the friendship that prompted Tasso to dedicate De amicitia to his patron. Finally, the poem mentions that Diodati had Italian ancestry—"et Tuscus tu quoque Damon"—but the headnote reveals that, while his father came from Luca, Diodati was, in all other respects, an Englishman (127). It seems Milton may have looked to Diodati to serve as an English version of the learned audiences he encountered in Italy, and when he lost him he may have felt he had lost the only equivalent in his immediate personal circumstances for the Italian milieu he saw as conducive to his literary ambitions.

Without some English equivalent for the private academies of Italy, Milton seemingly could not envision an institutional context for the production and reception and continual dissemination of epic. In 1642, therefore, tragedy seems the most promising of the three genres Milton considers. There are scriptural examples of the form, as there are also for epic and ode, but tragedy has a claim to be the preeminent genre, as ode does not, and Milton can at least envision circumstances for the reception and perpetuation of a tragedy, as he cannot yet do for epic. Viewed in this way, it is not entirely surprising that Milton temporarily abandoned his long-standing plans to write a heroic poem, and that almost all of the entries in the Trinity Manuscript are plans for tragedies.

One should expect, then, that Milton's eventual return to epic designs would be motivated at least in part by some development in the institutions by which literary works are perpetuated. Of course, September 1642 saw one very dramatic change in the institutions of literary circulation: Parliament's closing of the theaters. In itself this need not have altered Milton's inclination toward the genre of tragedy. He had not envisioned himself writing for the commercial stage, but for a reformed stage; and he might for a while have convinced himself that Parliament was closing the commercial stage so as to "take into their [own] care...the managing of [England's] publick sports and festival pastimes," as he had suggested in *The Reason of Church Government* that they do (CM 3.1:239).

But a year later, when Parliament went even further than suppressing the commercial theater and passed an ordinance for licensing the press, Milton surely could not have believed there was much likelihood of Parliament taking such an enlightened and proactive role in cultural affairs.[9] *Areopagitica* includes no expression of hope for a state-sponsored theater, even though there is an appropriate moment in Milton's argument for discussing such a possibility. When elaborating on the inevitable ineffectiveness of the law Parliament has passed, Milton claims that the great art of government lies in being able "to discern in what the law is to bid restraint and punishment, and in what things perswasion only is to work" (CM 4.318–19). Had he harbored any lingering hopes of a state-sponsored theater, enticing Englishmen to more virtuous private and civic behavior, this reference to governments controlling their citizens through inducements as well as punishments would have afforded Milton the opportunity to remind Parliament of his suggestion that they procure "artfull recitations sweetened with eloquent and gracefull inticements to the love and practice of justice, temperance, and fortitude" (CM 3.1:240).

The School as Site of Canonical Reproduction

That he included no such reminder indicates that by 1644 Milton clearly no longer believed it likely that the parliamentary government would institute a theater conducive to his literary ambitions. But while this disappointment might have made him reconsider his inclination toward tragedy, it does not yet provide a positive motive for preferring epic. That, I believe, was provided by another institutional development in England during the early 1640s: the educational reforms initiated by Samuel Hartlib and his circle. In the period between the publication of *The Reason of Church Government* and *Areopagitica*, Milton's involvement in England's educational scene (through his taking on of pupils and his composition of an educational treatise) might have suggested to him that the school was an appropriate institution for the perpetuation of his literary works.

Milton's vision of an ideal school was (as his vision of an ideal theater had been) in part a vision of an institution in which the sort of literary work he aimed to produce might be perpetuated. In the educational system sketched in *Of Education*, he makes the study of heroic poems, tragedies, histories, and political orations the penultimate focus for his students (the ultimate focus was learning how to *compose* such works). In Milton's school, students would be expected to memorize and recite passages from these works: "When all these employments are well conquer'd, then will the choise histories, *heroic poems*, and *Attic* tragedies, of statliest and most regal argument, with all the famous Politicall orations offer themselves; which, if they were not only read, but some of them got by memory and solemly pronounc't with right accent, and grace, as might be taught, would endue them even with the spirit, and vigor of *Demosthenes* or *Cicero, Euripides* or *Sophocles*" (CM 4.285–86). The care afforded to literature in such a program suggests that Milton's practical experience with teaching allowed him to consider the school as a setting in which his future poetic works might be disseminated and perpetuated.

This passage, though, might suggest that Milton was still inclined to compose in the genre of tragedy, for he mentions particular tragedians by name. But in this context that may be for no other reason than that speeches from plays are written to be spoken aloud and thus make more natural recitation exercises. For he also mentions Demosthenes and Cicero, even though he certainly does not regard political orations in prose, "a mortal thing, of no Empyreall conceit," as the kind of literature he intends to leave to aftertimes. In any case, he has begun to imagine the school as an institution to which he might entrust the survival of his literary works.[10]

Unfortunately, between the period when he wrote *Of Education* and the time, probably in 1658, when he committed himself to the composition of an epic, Milton left little evidence regarding his deliberations over the genre of his proposed poems. However, in the years immediately prior to 1658, several publications provided him with an opportunity to refine his thoughts on the matter—especially in regard to the institutions that might contribute to the survival of his work. The year 1656 saw the publication of an epic and a drama by two prominent former royalists whose artistic abilities Milton seems to have admired despite their politics: Davenant's *Seige of Rhodes* was performed and published, and the opening books of Cowley's never-to-be-completed epic *Davideis* appeared in his *Poems*.

Milton's interest in music and his own probable exposure to opera during his continental tour might have generated in him an interest in Davenant's attempts to introduce recitative drama into English culture. What he learned of the play, though, would no doubt have disappointed Milton. Although the story of Alphonso, Ianthe, and the Turk Solyman by no means contains the scandalous licentiousness characteristic of Restoration drama (Davenant considered himself to be writing a heroic drama), the production revived elements of the old court masques, especially the elaborate scenery frequently changed during the course of the performance.[11] Insofar as Milton took Davenant's performance as signaling the possibility of a revival of theatrical institutions in England, I believe it would have dissuaded him from committing to the composition of "*Attic* tragedies, of statliest and most regal argument." First, the very survival of the theater Davenant was attempting to resurrect must have seemed in 1656 highly questionable. And second, Milton would have regarded such a theater, even if it did survive, as unsuitable for his version of heroic drama.

In the same year, however, Milton was able to compare with Davenant's drama an example of the other major genre in which he had long contemplated composing. Cowley's *Poems,* including the first four books of his biblical epic, *Davideis,* appeared in 1656. Several features of Cowley's book, including the institution with which commentators connected it, might have made it seem preferable in Milton's estimation to what he learned of Davenant's drama—and preferable also as a guide to his own poetic ambitions. First, certain aspects of Cowley's aesthetic philosophy might have made *Davideis* attractive to Milton; Cowley speaks as follows in his preface:

> When I consider this [the story of David] and how many other bright and magnificent subjects of the like nature the holy Scripture affords and proffers, as it were, to poesy; in the wise managing and illustrating whereof the glory of God Almighty might be joined with the singular utility and noblest delight of mankind, it is not without grief and indignation that I behold that divine science employing all her inexhaustible riches of wit and eloquence, either in the wicked and beggarly flattery of great persons, or the unmanly idolizing of foolish women, or the wretched affectation of scurril laughter, or at best on the confused antiquated dreams of senseless fables and metamorphoses.[12]

How well this accords with Milton's view that the "frequent songs throughout the law and prophets" excel those of Greece and Rome, "not in their divine argument alone, but in the very critical art of composition," and that skill in poetic ability is "of power beside the office of a pulpit, to imbreed and cherish in a great people the seeds of vertu and publick civility" (CM 3.1:238). How nearly it conforms to Milton's sense of "what despicable creatures our common Rimers and Playwriters be, and...what Religious, what glorious and magnificent use might be made of Poetry, both in divine and humane things" (CM 4.286). How eagerly would Milton have seconded Cowley's question, "Why will not the actions of Sampson afford as plentiful matter as the labours of Hercules?"

But beyond these general points of aesthetic agreement between Milton and Cowley, the institutional site of reception for the *Davideis* might have confirmed Milton in his sense that academic institutions could serve to promote the survival of literary works. Of course, Cowley's work was generally popular. As Loiseau says, with the publication of *Poems*, Cowley came to stand "in the eyes of his contemporaries, not only as the greatest English poet then living, and one of the greatest England had ever known, with Shakespeare and Spenser, but even as the worthy successor and rival of the supreme masters of the craft, the Ancients. The soul of Virgil and Homer was felt to breathe anew in the *Davideis*."[13]

But beyond the general esteem that Loiseau details, the work was also conspicuously associated with academic institutions. A 1658 burlesque of contemporary poetry called *Naps upon Parnassus* playfully mocked the work: "Cowley's alack's too plain; his Davideis, / But fit for boyes to read, like Virgil's Enoeis."[14] And if the ode by Oxford student Thomas Sprat welcoming Cowley's book into the Bodleian Library is any indication, perhaps the *Davideis* did quickly become an object of study in the schools.[15] Insofar as his own teaching of "boyes" had begun to suggest to Milton that schools might be the appropriate venue for the reception, dissemination, and perpetuation of his work, the fate of Cowley's truncated epic must have encouraged him in this belief. Cowley had closed his preface to the poem as follows: "I shall be ambitious of no other fruit from this weak and imperfect attempt of mine, but the opening of a way to the courage and industry of some other persons, who may be better able to perform it thoroughly and successfully." Perhaps one respect in which Cowley "opened the way" for Milton was by confirming that there was, in the school, an institution that could ensure the survival of vernacular epic poetry.

Milton had, after all, remained interested in issues of education even after the publication of his small treatise on the matter. He continued to take on students, such as Lady Ranelagh's son and Thomas Ellwood, right up to the eve of the Restoration. In 1654, in his *Second Defense,* he urged Cromwell to "make a better provision for the education and morals of youth, than has been made" (CM 8.237). In *The Likeliest Means to Remove Hirelings* of 1659, he suggests that England "erect in greater number all over the land schooles and competent libraries to those schooles" (CM 6.80) And, on the verge of the Restoration, in *The Ready and Easy Way,* he sketches in some detail the kinds of schools and academies that the gentry might establish in each county of England (CM 6.145). Indeed, given the urgency with which Milton rushed this last pamphlet into print, his relatively detailed treatment of schools suggests that he may have felt one of the main failings of the Interregnum governments had been in the realm of education.

Given that Milton remained interested in England's educational scene throughout the 1650s, there are two publications in the later years of that decade that might have made an impression on him just as he was beginning composition of his epic. In 1657, Comenius's *Opera didactica omnia,* which included his *Didactica magna,* was published, followed, in 1658, by his *Orbus pictus.*

Paradise Lost as School Text

Milton, cognizant of the aforementioned developments in the institutions of canonical reproduction, chose the genre of epic and composed *Paradise Lost* with schools and universities in mind as the sites in which his work would be received, appreciated, and perpetuated. The epic itself exhibits signs of this orientation. Stanley Fish argues that reading the epic is an educative experience. Mary Ann Radzinowicz demonstrates that the narratorial persona of *Paradise Lost* is that of a teacher. Ann Baynes Coiro notes that Adam's education by Michael in the closing books of the epic is closely modeled on the educational plan set out in *Of Education*. Anna K. Nardo examines two "academic interludes" in the epic, inspired by Milton's critical acquaintance with the Italian academies. Barbara K. Lewalski notes, "*Paradise Lost* is unique among the great epics in that a good half of it presents formal schemes of education." Richard J. DuRocher details the influence that Latin texts taught by Milton to his nephews and other boys had on passages in his epic. And Margaret Thickstun shows how appropriate the issues raised within *Paradise Lost* are to college-age students.[16] Such arguments, however, concern only the subject matter or general purpose of the epic. My argument is more specific: Milton designed *Paradise Lost* to be received, and used, within a particular educational environment.

Consider first Milton's own brief but suggestive description of his envisioned audience. In the proem to book 7, he expresses his hope that his poem will a "fit audience find, though few" (*PL* 7.31). The word *fit* is one that seems directly connected in Milton's mind to education. In *Of Education*, Milton calls "a compleat and generous Education that which fits a man to perform justly, skillfully and magnanimously all the offices, both private and publick, of Peace and War" (CM 4.280). In *The Ready and Easy Way*, written at the same time that he was composing *Paradise Lost*, he claims that to "make the people fittest to chuse, and the chosen fittest to govern" will "mend our corrupt and faulty education" (CM 6.132).

Consider second that *Paradise Lost* contains the kinds of "lectures and explanations" that Milton in *Of Education* recommends be used to encourage students as they begin their studies: such "as may lead and draw [students] in willing obedience, enflam'd with the study of Learning, and the admiration of Vertue" (CM 4.282). One can imagine a teacher in a Miltonic academy exhorting his pupils, as Raphael does Adam, that "Heav'n / Is as the Book of God before thee set, / Wherein to read his wondrous Works, and learne / His Seasons, Hours, or Dayes, or Months, or Yeares" (*PL* 8.66–69). Or, more broadly, one can imagine students using *Paradise Lost* like a textbook. Consider the epic's affinities to the earliest school textbooks. According to historian of education James Bowen, the publication of Comenius's *Orbis pictus* in 1658 in Germany (1659 in England) "initiated a tradition of school textbooks designed to be put in the hands of the children themselves."[17] And certain passages in *Paradise Lost* formally resemble material in the *Orbis*—in particular the passages in which a series of proper or common nouns are rapidly listed, with perhaps an adjective or brief comment: "Scorpion and Asp, and *Amphisbaena* dire, / *Cerastes* hornd, *Hydrus*, and *Ellops* drear, / And *Dipsas*" (10.524–26). Milton's list seems a sophisticated version of the one a young student would encounter in the *Orbus*, under the category of "Serpents and Creeping Things":

> *Snakes* creep by winding themselves;
> The *Adder*, in the wood;
> The *Water-snake* in the water;
> The *Viper*, among great stones.
> The *Asp* in the fields.
> The *Boa*, (or Mild-snake) in Houses.
> The *Slow-worm* is blind.
> The *Lizard*, and the *Salamander* (that liveth long in fire) have
>   feet.
> The *Dragon, a winged Serpent*, killeth with his Breath.
> The *Basilisk*, with his Eyes;
> And the *Scorpion*, with his poysonous tail.[18]

The greater sophistication of Milton's lines results from the fact that the passage from Comenius is for students just beginning their studies, while Milton would have students study heroic poems at age 20 or 21. But Milton envisions that, all during their education, students "for memories sake [will] retire back into the middle ward, and sometimes into the rear of what they have been taught, untill they have confirm'd and solidly united the whole body of their perfeted knowledge" (CM 4.287). *Paradise Lost* provides students with the opportunity to do precisely that in passages like the one cited above (such as, "Review the varieties of snakes") and in more expansive catalogs like the description of Creation in book 7. There we encounter "The Female Bee who feeds her Husband Drone"; the English *Orbis pictus* informs students that "The *Bee*, maketh honey which the *Drone* devoureth" (*PL* 7.490; *Orbis* 31). I am not arguing for Comenius as the source of Milton's conception; it is a commonplace. I only wish to document a similarity in form between portions of *Paradise Lost* and the earliest textbooks, and to suggest, on the basis of that similarity, that Milton envisioned his epic being received, disseminated, studied, and perpetuated in schools.[19]

Having mentioned students of various ages, I might return to one final piece of external evidence for the argument I am advancing. The first person to whom Milton showed the whole text of *Paradise Lost* was Thomas Ellwood. Ellwood might seem an unusual choice, given that Milton counted among his acquaintances someone with as subtle an aesthetic sensibility as Andrew Marvell. But if Milton wanted to determine whether his epic might serve as the penultimate experience in a liberal education, Ellwood was perhaps the most appropriate person of Milton's acquaintance to whom to show the work. Ellwood was 25 years old when in 1665 he was given *Paradise Lost* to read, a bit older than the oldest student Milton imagines in his academy. But then Ellwood had come to Milton admitting that his schooling had been deficient, so perhaps Milton thought him, at 25, the equivalent of a 21 year old who had been well educated from the start of his academic career. Or perhaps Milton was thinking of Ellwood's age in 1659, and hoping to gauge from his response to the epic whether this kind of work, published earlier, might have trained up a population fit to have prevented the restoration of "*Bacchus* and his revellers" (*PL* 7.33).

In any case, within the late republic and early Restoration milieux, Milton seems to have felt that schools might serve to receive, value, disseminate, and perpetuate his literary work. (In what must have seemed to him a somewhat promising development, the so-called dissenting academies began to be founded at almost the same time as the initial publication of *Paradise Lost*.) Presciently anticipating the canonizing role of the school that soon emerged, as Guillory has shown, Milton channeled his literary ambitions into a work that students might profitably encounter near the culmination of their formal education—precisely where most readers of *Paradise Lost* today do encounter the work, once the "steddy pace of [their] learning" has prepared them to appreciate his "true Epic Poem."

Conclusion

Near the end of her comprehensive consideration of the dynamics of canon formation, Barbara Herrnstein Smith summarizes, in very broad strokes, her treatment of the factors that determine a work's canonical fortunes: "Any object or artifact that performs certain desired/able functions particularly well at a given time for some community of subjects...will have an immediate survival advantage," for it will be "more frequently read or recited, copied or reprinted, translated, cited, imitated and commented upon—in short, culturally re-produced." As a result, "it will be more available to perform those or other functions for other subjects at a subsequent time." She continues by tracing the "two possible trajectories [that] may ensue" for such a literary artifact. It may be that "under the changing and emergent conditions of that subsequent time, the functions for which the text was earlier valued are no longer desired/able," or that those functions are "better served by...newly produced" works, in which case, the work will be "less well maintained and less frequently cited and recited so that its visibility as well as its interest will fade." Alternately, if "under changing conditions and in competition with newly produced and re-produced works, it continues to perform *some* desired/able functions particularly well, even if not the same ones for which it was initially valued...it will continue to be cited and recited, continue to be available to succeeding generations of subjects."[1]

A formulation like this rightly corrects the naïve notion that canonical texts owe their survival to specifiable intrinsic qualities, of universal significance or appeal, that are incorporated into them as a result of their authors' genius and then simply recognized by successive generations of readers. Instead, it puts the emphasis on cultural work done within the "changing and emergent conditions of...subsequent time," work that has as its result the perpetuation of particular literary texts. As Smith says elsewhere, "the value of a literary work is continuously produced and re-produced by the very acts of implicit and explicit evaluation that are frequently invoked as 'reflecting' its value and therefore as being evidence of it. In other words, what are commonly taken to be the *signs* of literary value are, in effect, also its *springs*."[2]

As is evident in the quotations above, underlying Smith's account of canon formation is the same general conception of culture that has enabled the historicist interpretive enterprise prominent within literary studies since the 1980s: namely, that each "community of subjects...at a given time" constitutes a discrete phenomenon available for synchronic cultural analysis, and that history (even the ongoing history of a particular nation) is most fruitfully regarded as a succession of individual historical "moments"—effectively, distinct cultures. And in such an account, canonicity is repeatedly conferred (if it is, or withheld) extrinsically; the agents of canonization are those discrete, subsequent cultures.

In at least some versions of this view, moreover, the difference between one culture and another regarding issues of literary status is presented as potentially radical and absolute. Terry Eagleton offers his version of Smith's theoretical principle and then illustrates with a startling hypothesis:

> The so-called "literary canon," the unquestioned "great tradition" of the "national literature," has to be regarded as a *construct*, fashioned by particular people for particular reasons at a certain time. There is no such thing as a literary work or tradition that is valuable *in itself*, regardless of what anyone

might have said or come to say about it. "Value" is a transitive term: it means whatever is valued by certain people in specific situations, according to particular criteria and in the light of given purposes. It is thus quite possible that, given a deep enough transformation of our history, we may in the future produce a society which is unable to get anything at all out of Shakespeare. His works might seem desperately alien, full of styles of thought and feeling which such a society found limited or irrelevant. In such a situation, Shakespeare would be no more valuable than much present-day graffiti.[3]

The prevailing critical premise, then, is that a given work's canonical status must be reproduced in each successive historical moment, and that this might be done in significantly, even radically, different ways in different geographical locations and at different moments on the historical continuum.

The source for this image of history, incidentally, as involving abrupt discontinuities, one synchronic moment to the next, is probably Foucault. In *The Order of Things*, for example, he describes and accounts for the "suddenness and thoroughness with which certain sciences were sometimes reorganized," how "within a few years (around 1800) the tradition of general grammar was replaced by an essentially historical philology; natural classifications were ordered according to the analyses of comparative anatomy; and a political economy was founded whose main themes were labour and production," and therefore the "space of knowledge" was "arranged in a totally different way."[4] Synchronism is more than just an analytical tool for recent historicist studies; it is an image of the actual workings of history.

In accounts of the process of canon formation based on such a historicist paradigm, the work's original author figures hardly at all. The titles of Daniel Javitch's study of the canonization of *Orlando Furioso* (*Proclaiming a Classic*) and Gary Taylor's examination of Shakespeare's status across cultures (*Reinventing Shakespeare*) are revealing; canonicity is externally conferred by the efforts of readers, critics, and theorists in the generations following the publication of a work.[5] The author plays no crucial role in the process. Perhaps the author is imagined as naïvely and futilely endowing his or her work with its (canonically nonfunctional) intrinsic qualities. No works of literature are born great, in this view; they all have greatness thrust upon 'em.

But what are we to make of an author like Milton, who deliberately set out to write a canonical work of literature, who seems to have had distinct ideas about what was involved in that process, *and who succeeded?* (As Stephen Fallon says, "Milton, as it has turned out, was prophetic about the afterlife of his works.")[6] Does his practical success in ensuring the survival of his literary masterpieces for 350 years entitle this author to a greater degree of consideration than an account of canon-formation as a wholly extrinsic process generally accords to authors?

Milton seems, after all, to have anticipated one of the key premises of contemporary canon theorists themselves: "written to aftertimes." The plural is significant. Milton does not imagine the future into which he sends his works as some undifferentiated "posterity," but—much as Smith, Eagleton, and others do—as a succession of distinct historical moments, each passing its own judgment on his work. He wants to leave something "so written to aftertimes, as they should not willingly let it die." His masterpieces are imagined, in effect, as being perpetually on life support, with any given generation capable of deciding to pull the plug. In this he would seem to have anticipated even Eagleton's sense of the possibility for radical evaluative difference from one generation to the next.

But, contrary to the contemporary understanding of the process of canon formation, Milton also seems to have believed that the author's own efforts could play an important role in his works' endurance. He did more than idly hope that "aftertimes" would not willingly let his works die; he believed he could, and resolved to, leave something "so written" that they would not do so. I have examined a number of the canonical calculations Milton made: that readers would remain interested in moral exempla; that they would be fascinated by an effort to reconcile biblical content with pagan form in a Christian epic; that there would be a special status accorded works perceived as "original" or "sublime"; that the institution of the school would undertake the perpetuation and dissemination of literary texts.

As the canon theorists would predict, these mechanisms of canonization have operated with differing degrees of efficacy in the various historical moments through which Milton's works have survived. Consider exemplarity, Milton's "faining notable images of vertues [and] vices."[7] Addison seems to have a straightforward appreciation of this dimension of the epic's moral design; he remarks that Abdiel, for example, "preserv[ing] his allegiance to his Maker, exhibits to us a noble moral of religious singularity."[8] As late as Samuel Johnson, pointed illustrations of virtuous and vicious behavior are treated as an expected and valuable aspect of the epic; among his remarks on the characters of Adam and Eve, for example, he observes, "when they have sinned, they shew how discord begins in mutual frailty, and how it ought to cease in mutual forbearance."[9] But, beginning perhaps with the Romantics, literary taste on moral exempla began to change. John Keats claimed to hate any poetry that had "a palpable design upon us." And William Blake famously read against the grain of Milton's exemplary scheme when he found the poet "of the devil's party."[10] Readers now generally prefer that authors not engineer and guide a moral evaluation of a story's characters. Contemporary Western sensibilities on such matters are well reflected in Chekov's letter to Aleksey Suvorin concerning authorial moral objectivity: "You would have me say, in depicting horse thieves, that stealing horses is an evil. But then, that has been known a long while, even without me. Let Jurors judge them, for my business is only to show them as they are."[11] Few readers probably now pick up *Paradise Lost* sincerely hoping to be taught "of sanctity and virtu through all the instances of example," even if for at least a century and a half such exempla represented a much valued dimension of the epic (CM 3:293).

As we have lost our taste for moral exempla, we moderns similarly may in large measure have lost our taste for the sublime. Since the nineteenth century, the dominant literary genre has been the realistic novel, and twentieth and twenty-first century literature has steered even further from the sublime through a minimalist impulse evident from Ernest Hemingway to Raymond Carver. But, as Leslie Moore states, "no other pairing—'sublime' and 'Milton'—[was] used more frequently in early discussions of the poet and *Paradise Lost*."[12] For a century and a half, it was under the category of "the sublime" that Milton's epic was chiefly valued. As Dustin Griffin puts it, "Milton was invariably cited, from Addison to Johnson, as England's great sublime poet, and *Paradise Lost* as the poem whose 'characteristick quality' is sublimity.[13]

Perhaps more consistently through the centuries that separate us from Milton, his determined effort to supply the Renaissance desideratum of a "Christian epic" has also helped to ensure the survival of his epic. In his gloss on Milton's invocation of the "Heav'nly Muse," Patrick Hume notes, "the poets, Ancient and Modern, in the beginning of their most Considerable Works at least, call some one, or all, the Muses to their Assistance." He cites the invocations of Homer and Virgil, then observes:

> As our Author has attempted a greater Undertaking than that of either of those two Master-Poets, so he had need invoke this Heavenly Muse, whom a little after he explains by God's Holy Spirit, to inspire and assist him: And well he might, being to sing, not only of the Beauteous Universe, and all Created Beings, but of the Creator Himself, and all those Revelations and Dispensations He had been pleased to make to Faln Man through the Great Redeemer of the World, His Son. This Argument might need a Divine Instructress, preferable to any of their Invoked Assistants.[14]

Johnson similarly admired the accomplishment represented in Milton's Christianizing of the epic genre:

The subject of an epic poem is naturally an event of great importance. That of Milton is not the destruction of a city, the conduct of a colony, or the foundation of an empire. His subject is the fate of worlds, the revolutions of heaven and of earth; rebellion against the Supreme King raised by the highest order of created beings; the overthrow of their host and the punishment of their crime; the creation of a new race of reasonable creatures; their original happiness and innocence, their forfeiture of immortality and their restoration to hope and peace.[15]

And while students' knowledge both of classical literature and of the Bible is on the wane, the accomplishment represented by successfully composing a "Christian epic" remains one of the grounds through which the canonical status of *Paradise Lost* is maintained to this day. In *The Riverside Milton*, Flannagan devotes the first and most extensive section of his introduction to *Paradise Lost* to detailing the tradition of epic, commenting that Milton "uses all the obvious epic devices, but he significantly rejects epic themes and devices he feels are beneath Christian epic."[16]

The concept of "originality" also continues to function as a discursive mechanism of canonization for *Paradise Lost*. Indeed, the canonizing force of this concept has perhaps only increased over the centuries. In the late seventeenth century, the term *original* might still have a mildly pejorative force. The *Oxford English Dictionary* gives one contemporary definition as "a singular, odd, or eccentric person." But John Dennis's 1704 claim that *Paradise Lost* is "an Original Poem; that is to say, a Poem that should have his own Thoughts, his own Images, and his own Spirit," sounds unambiguously laudatory. And the *Longman Anthology of British Literature*, for instance, continues to use the term as an established honorific: "Milton draws on the Bible, Homer, Virgil and Dante to create his own original sound and story."[17]

Of all of Milton's canonical calculations, entrusting the perpetuation of his epic to the institution of the school is what at present undoubtedly has the most powerful impact on the canonicity of his epic. Through the eighteenth and nineteenth centuries, *Paradise Lost* was perhaps simply read by the "common reader." But through the twentieth century and into the twenty-first, it has been a school text. As a result, an interpretive industry Milton might scarcely have been able to imagine has grown up around the poem. Every explicit defense of *Paradise Lost* within the "canon wars" of the 1980s naturally had a direct impact on the canonicity of the text. But every interpretation that simply *assumes* the value of the epic—as well as the very existence of a Milton Society, *Milton Studies*, and *Milton Quarterly*—also contributes, implicitly but significantly, to the canonical status of Milton's literary works.

I have argued that, by observing how the Homeric epics were being canonically reproduced in his own day, Milton wrote *Paradise Lost* in an attempt to exploit the same discursive and institutional mechanisms of canonization, and that these aspects of its composition go a long way toward accounting for the endurance of Milton's epic through the centuries. I will conclude by considering an even more fundamental aspect of Milton's relation to Homer and the bearing it has on the canonical status of *Paradise Lost*. Milton's epic explicitly asks its readers to evaluate the poem relative to the *Iliad*, the *Odyssey*, and other classical epics. He declares his intention to soar "*above* th'Aonian mount" and claims that his epic sings a "*better* fortitude" than the one celebrated in pagan epic. While every epic seeks to surpass its predecessors—indeed, while this ambition is itself an expected topos of the genre—Milton's proems (unprecedented additions to an epic poem, for which he incurred the censure of Johnson) explicitly ask the reader to rank *Paradise Lost* relative to earlier epics. They invite the reader into the very activity—judging, evaluating, prioritizing—by which the literary canon is established.

"So written to aftertimes, as they should not *willingly* let it die": it should perhaps be no surprise that the author whose master theme was choice should imagine the survival of his literary works as being a function of subsequent readers' wills. John

Guillory downplays the role of evaluative judgment in the constitution of the literary canon: "I would like to suggest that the
question of judgment is the wrong question to raise in the context
of canon-formation. The selection of texts for preservation certainly does presuppose acts of judgment, which are indeed complex psychic and social events; but these acts are necessary rather
than sufficient to constitute a process of canon-formation."[18] For
Guillory, more fundamental social matters determine the constitution of the canon: "the reason for the absence of great works
by women before the eighteenth century (not after) is in fact very
easy to determine: there were few women *writers* before this
time." As a result, "what the [early] critics of the canon took to
be exclusion from a final, immutable selection of great texts was
really, in historical context, exclusion from the means of literary
production, from *literacy* itself." For Guillory, "in order to understand the historical circumstances determining the constitution
of the literary canon, then, we must see its history as the history of both the production and the reception of texts. We must
understand that the history of literature is not only a question of
what we read but of *who* reads and *who* writes, and in what social
circumstances."[19]

But, as valid and salutary as Guillory's perspective is in explain-
ing what on the surface appear to be reprehensible exclusions of
particular groups from the literary canon, nevertheless, in order
to account for the particular texts that are *included* in a canon,
we must return to those "necessary rather than sufficient" acts
of judgment. Canon-making necessarily involves evaluating,
judging, and ranking. And it may be no small source of Milton's
canonical status that he explicitly engages readers in such an
evaluative response to his works and thematizes such activity in
them.

As Milton imagines it, choosing is not simply a matter of
selecting, at a particular moment, one's preference from roughly
equal alternatives. Nor is it a matter of opting for an easily recognized good over an easily recognized evil. It involves prioritizing,

ranking things that are themselves intrinsically good, but comparatively superior and inferior. Adam's sin is characterized as a failure to prioritize properly: "Was shee thy God?" Moreover, choosing is imagined as an ongoing activity, and one that has the effect of maintaining an existing state. The choice that God provides Adam and Eve is not a this-or-that option presented to them at a particular moment, but takes the form of a prohibition, which means that for as long as they do not violate his command they are choosing aright, as a continuous, ongoing act. And they keep a paradise in existence as a result.

In our historical moment, in this particular "aftertime," we have become (perhaps rightly) tentative about making evaluative judgments; the grounds for such judgments have been exposed as neither natural nor commonsensical nor universal, but as tending to serve the interests of the privileged. We are, moreover (perhaps rightly), uneasy regarding the conservative dimension of the philological enterprise; we hesitate to carry forward particular texts if that should involve carrying forward structures of oppression with which those texts were complicit. And yet Milton understood (rightly) that there is no escape from evaluation, judging, choosing—that, as T. S. Eliot puts it, "criticism is as inevitable as breathing." Unlike Dante's, Milton's cosmos does not include a region for the uncommitted. One must choose; one is always choosing something. And Milton further understood that to persist in a right choosing, not willingly to let some things die, is to keep a paradise in existence.

Appendix

Milton's Homer

Particularly for an argument like the one in this book—that Milton's allusions to Homer should be interpreted in light of the contemporary understanding of the Homeric passage evoked—it would be useful to know the edition of Homer from which Milton worked. Miltonists once felt confident that Milton worked from Spondanus's edition of 1583. Harris Francis Fletcher, working from marginal references to Homer thought to be in Milton's hand in an edition of Pindar, showed that the page numbers in those references corresponded to the Spondanus edition. In 1964, however, Maurice Kelley and Samuel D. Atkins argued that the Spondanus references were not in Milton's hand, and could not, therefore, serve as evidence for Milton's owning and using Spondanus's edition. Their view has not been challenged. But neither have any new grounds emerged for identifying the edition of Homer from which Milton worked.

I have unfortunately not been able to find any other evidence that would help determine the edition of Homer from which Milton worked. In this appendix, I will report the results of two unsuccessful efforts I have made to do so, in the hopes that, although I am only mapping two dead ends, I may have cleared brush that will eventually lead someone to glimpse a viable path to the goal.

Within his Latin prose, Milton three times cites Homer, with the Homeric phrase translated into Latin. In the *Defensio pro populo anglicano*, he cites *Iliad* 1.238–39 (δικασπολοι, ηοιτε τηεμιστας / προς Διος ειρυαται), providing as a Latin translation "judices qui leges / ab Jove custodunt." At another spot, he quotes Achilles's condemnation of Agamemnon as "Populi vorator rex, quoniam hominibus nihili imperas. / Alioqui enim Atrida, nunc postremum inuriam faceres" (444). In the *Defensio secunda*, he cites *Iliad* 9.411–16, and then provides the following translation:

> Duplicia fata ducere ad mortis finem:
> Si hic manens circa Troum urban pugnavero,
> Amittitur mihi reditus; sed Gloria immortalis erit,
> Si domum revertor dulce ad Patrium solum,
> Amittitur mihi Gloria pulchra, sed diuturna vita
> Erit.

Many of the editions of Homer in the early modern period provided a facing page Latin translation. If the Latin translations of Homeric passages in Milton's prose were all found to correspond to one of these Latin translations, it would be a good sign that that edition was the one Milton used. Of course, we know full well that Milton could produce his own translation, and he might have preferred to do so, translating the phrases in a way that best served his immediate argumentative purposes. But if, in the rush of constructing his argument, he did not bother to do so, but just drew on a translation near to hand, we might have evidence of the edition from which he read Homer.

Unfortunately, however, none of the major editions of Homer available to Milton render the Latin precisely as it is translated in his defenses. I have examined 24 editions, but will illustrate my points with five of the most prominent ones. In the passages on judges, Milton's translation, again, is "judices qui leges / ab Jove custodunt." The Stephanus edition of 1567 translates "iudices, quiq[ue] leges / A Ioue hauserunt." The E. Vignon edition of 1574 renders the phrase as "iudices, quique leges / A Ioue tuentur." The Spondanus edition of 1583 and 1606 has the lines as "iudices, quique leges / A Ioue acceptas." A 1632 edition annotated edition of the first four books of the *Iliad* does use the same verb Milton chooses, but uses a different word for *laws:* "iudices, qui iura / a Iove custodiunt." An edition published at Cambridge in 1648 perhaps comes closest to Milton, rendering the phrase as "judices, quique leges / A Jove traditas custodiunt," though even here there is not an exact match because of the added "traditas."

In the somewhat longer quotation of Achilles's condemnation of Agamemnon, we again do not find translations that accord perfectly with Milton's. For comparison, let me repeat Milton's phrasing: "Populi vorator rex, quoniam hominibus nihili imperas. / Alioqui enim Atrida, nunc postremum inuriam faceres." The Stephanus edition gives "Populivorator rex, quoniam uiribus imperas. / Certe enim Atride nunc postremum damnum intulisses." Vignon has "Populivorator Rex: quoniam ignauis imperas / Certe enim Atride postremam hanc contumeliam fecisses." Stephanus renders the lines "Populivorator Rex, quoniam nullius pret[ii] hominib[us] imperas. / Certe enim Atrida, nunc postrema[m] co[n]tumelia[m] facere." The 1632 edition has "populi vorator rex, quando quidem nullius precii viris imperas / certe vero Atride nunc postremo contumeliosus fuisses," and the 1648 Cambridge edition has "Populi-devorator rex: nam ignauis imperas / Certe' enim, Atrida, nunc postremam intulisses istam contumeliam." Milton's translation is not particularly close to any of these renderings, most of which have "contumeliam" where he has "inuriam," and "certe" where he has "alioqui."

Finally, in the case of the "two fates" passage, Stephanus translates the passage as follows:

> Duas parcas ferre mortis ad finem.
> Siquide illic manens Troianoru ciuitate circa pugnaro,
> Peribit quidem mihi reditus, sed gloria incorrupta erit:
> Quod si domum revertar dilectam in patriam terram,
> Peribit mihi gloria bona, superq, diu mihi aetas
> Erit.

E. Vignon renders the passage thus:

> Duas parcas ferre mortu ad finem
> Si manens hoc loco, ad urbem Troianorum pugnauero
> Peribit quidem mihi reditus, sed gloria immortalis erit
> Quod si domum revertar dilectam in patriam terram
> Peribit mihi gloria bona: diuturnum vero mihi aeuum
> Erit.

Spondanus gives:

> Duo fata ferre mortis ad finem.
> Si quide hic manes Troianoru civutatem circa pugnauero
> Perijt quidem mihi reditus: sed gloria immortalis erit
> Quod si domum reuertar dilectam in patria terram
> Perijt mihi gloria bona: in diuturnum tempus autem aetas
> Erit.

For this passage, the edition of the *Iliad* published at Cambridge in 1648 offers the same translation as Spondanus. As for the translation Milton provides in *Defensio secunda*, phrases where that rendering resembles the Latin translation in any of the major Renaissance editions of Homer more than another ("sed gloria immortalis erit" instead of "sed gloria incorrupta erit") fall within the range of expectation of two translators rendering a particular passage independently.

Unfortunately, then, Milton's own direct citations of Homer have not helped me to identify the edition of Homer from which he worked.

A second possible route to that goal has similarly proven unfruitful. In working with Milton's allusions, I encountered a number for which, in converting the Greek spur to his own English reprise, Milton altered the Homeric phrasing in a way that the immediate context of his own poem did not seem to necessitate. Of course, an alluding author is at liberty to make whatever alterations he or she might wish to the spur, but for this set of allusions, I could not make out a motivation for Milton's changes, which made me wonder whether his allusion might be based on a typographical error in the Homeric text from which he was working, or if the non-Homeric element of his allusion was suggested to him by the commentary in an annotated edition like that of Spondanus. If the distinctive and unwarranted change in a whole set of reprises could be shown to derive from a set of typographical errors unique to one edition, or to the commentary in a particular annotated edition, that might serve as a kind of evidence for the edition from which Milton worked.

Let me give an example. In book 4, Milton describes the garden of Eden as follows: "underfoot the Violet, / Crocus, and Hyacinth with rich inlay / Broiderd the ground" (700–02). The Homeric spur for this line is a passage in book 14 of the *Iliad* where Zeus makes a plot of flowers to spring up as a bed for his and Hera's lovemaking: λωτόν θ᾽ ἑρσήεντα ἰδὲ κρόκον ἠδ᾽ ὑάκινθον (348), clover and daisies and crocuses and hyacinth. Milton has carried over Homer's crocuses and hyacinth, but exchanged clover and daisies for violets. He might have had any number of reasons for doing so. Perhaps there is some other, non-Homeric source for violets as an appropriate flower in paradise. Perhaps the word *violet* fit his meter better. Perhaps he just personally liked the look or smell of violets better than daisies or clover.

But one other possibility is that the edition of Homer from which he was working had some sort of misprint, the Greek word for violet (ιον) in the place of λωτόν, say. Or the commentary in an annotated edition for some reason mentioned violets, and Milton carried the notion into his verses from there. If so, we might have one tiny piece of evidence for the edition from which Milton worked. And, if a number of such instances were all to corresponded with unique elements of one particular edition, it might point to the edition Milton used, in the way that patterns of repeated scribal errors can help scholars track lines of manuscript transmission.

Here is my list of allusions where Milton's small and (to my eye) contextually unmotivated changes might, if they were to correspond to typographical errors or commentary unique to one particular edition, provide evidence for the edition of Homer from which he worked. At 1.560, he describes the angels as "Breathing united force" where the Homeric spur (*Iliad* 2.536, for example) just has "breathing force." At 2.548, the devils sing "thir own Heroic deeds"; in book 9, when the embassy reaches the retired Achilles, they find him singing "the famous deeds of men." Milton borrows Odysseus's "Hyacanthine Locks" for his description of Adam (*Odyssey* 6.231), but adds that they hung from his forelock in a "manly" fashion (4.302). In another reference to Zeus and Hera's lovemaking, Milton says Adam smiled toward Eve "as *Jupiter* / On *Juno* smiles, when he impregns the Clouds / That shed *May* Flowers" (4.499–501); in Homer, it is Zeus himself who causes the flowers to spring up, and then gathers a cloud around himself and Hera (14.346–51). Zeus has ambrosial hair (*Iliad* 1.529); the figure in Eve's dream has "dewy locks [that] *distill'd* /Ambrosia" (5.56). God's eyes are "unsleeping"; Zeus in the model passage just does not happen to be sleeping that particular night (5.647, *Iliad* 2.1). At 6.172, Abdiel says to Satan, "still thou errst, nor end wilt find / Of erring." In the Homeric spur, Hera says to Zeus, "you lie, nor will you put an end on (that is, bring to accomplishment) what you have said"; the word *end* is used very differently in each case (*Iliad* 19.107). The Homeric passage on which the "stream of Nectarous humor" of 6.332 is based has ἰχώρ rather than nectar (*Iliad* 5.340). Milton's "sacred Morn" is based on a line that mentions the dawn and then describes the *day* as "sacred" (6.748; *Iliad* 11.84).

Again, for each of these allusions, Milton might have made the change to the Homeric spur for any number of reasons. But if a number of his changes were found to have been suggested to him by typographical errors in a particular edition or glosses in a particular commentary, that could serve as evidence that Milton read from that edition. Unfortunately, I have found no such pattern of errors or glosses to suggest that Milton read from the Stephanus, Vignon, Spondanus, or Cambridge editions of the poem. That does not, of course, eliminate any of them as possibilities. But it means that the edition from which Milton read sadly remains as of yet unidentified.

NOTES

Notes to Introduction

1. Davis P. Harding, *The Club of Hercules* (Urbana: University of Illinois Press, 1962), 108; Charles Martindale, *John Milton and the Transformation of Ancient Epic* (London: Croon Helm, 1986), 79; William M. Porter, *Reading the Classics and "Paradise Lost"* (Lincoln: University of Nebraska Press, 1993), 94.

2. J. Milton French, ed., *Life Records of John Milton* (New Brunswick: Rutgers University Press, 1949–58), 5:110, 327–28.

3. Toland quoted in Helen Darbishire, *The Early Lives of Milton* (London: Constable, 1932), 179.

4. Richardson quoted in ibid., 290.

5. Samuel Johnson, *The Lives of the Most Eminent English Poets* (Oxford: Clarendon Press, 2006), 275.

6. Joseph Addison, *Critical Essays from "The Spectator,"* ed. Donald F. Bond (New York: Oxford University Press, 1970), 148.

7. Ibid., 80.

8. Johnson, *Lives,* 285, 292.

9. John Henry Todd, ed., *The Poetical Works of John Milton,* 4 vols. (London: Rivingtons, 1842).

10. John Milton, *The Reason of Church Government,* 3:1.236. All references to Milton's poetry and prose are to *The Works of John Milton,* ed. Frank Allen Patterson et al., 18 vols. (New York: Columbia University Press, 1931–40); hereafter cited as CM, followed by volume, part (in some cases), and page number. References to *Paradise Lost* will appear parenthetically in the text as *PL* by book and line number and are also from this edition.

11. Porter, *Reading the Classics,* 17, 21, 32–33, 30.

12. G. W. Pigman, "Varieties of Imitation in the Renaissance," *Renaissance Quarterly* 33 (Spring 1980): 2.

13. Ibid., 12.

14. *Odyssey* 11.489–91. Quotations from Homer are from the translations of Richmond Lattimore, *The Iliad of Homer* (Chicago: University

of Chicago Press, 1961; *The Odyssey of Homer* (New York: Harper & Row, 1975), both hereafter cited by book and line number. In cases where Lattimore's translation does not capture the element Milton is attempting to recall in his allusion, I provide the Greek text from *Homeri opera*, 4 vols., 3rd ed., ed. David T. Monroe and Thomas W. Allen (Oxford: Clarendon, 1920), and provide my own translation.

15. Porter, *Reading the Classics*, 90, 94.

16. Pigman, "Varieties of Imitation," 45.

17. Porter, *Reading the Classics*, 92.

18. Stephen Fallon, *Milton's Peculiar Grace: Self-Representation and Authority* (Ithaca: Cornell University Press, 2007), 221. Milton's desire for literary fame runs as a recurrent motif through this study of the poet's self-conception and self-presentation; see esp. 170–73.

19. Joseph Pucci, *The Full-Knowing Reader: Allusion and the Power of the Reader in the Western Literary Tradition* (New Haven: Yale University Press, 1998), x.

20. Jonathan Culler, "Presupposition and Intertextuality," *The Pursuit of Signs: Semiotics, Literature, Deconstruction* (Ithaca: Cornell University Press, 1981), 100, 103.

21. Julia Kristeva, *Revolution in Poetic Language*, trans. Margaret Waller (New York: Columbia University Press, 1984), 60.

22. Harold Bloom, *A Map of Misreading* (Oxford: Oxford University Press, 1975), 19, 17.

23. Louis Montrose, "Professing the Renaissance: The Poetics and Politics of Culture," in *The New Historicism*, ed. H. Aram Veeser (New York: Routledge, 1989), 17.

24. Stephen Dobranski, *Milton, Authorship and the Book Trade* (Cambridge: Cambridge University Press), 1999.

25. Annabel Patterson, *Reading between the Lines* (London: Routledge, 1993), 258.

Notes to Chapter 1

1. Edmund Spenser, *The Faerie Queene: Book One*, ed. Carol V. Kaske (Indianapolis: Hackett, 2006), 1.1.54.

2. Jonathan Culler, "Presupposition and Intertextuality," *The Pursuit of Signs: Semiotics, Literature, Deconstruction* (Ithaca: Cornell University Press, 1981), 109.

3. Harold Bloom, *A Map of Misreading* (Oxford: Oxford University Press, 1975), 19, 17.

4. Richard Garner, *From Homer to Tragedy: The Art of Allusion in Greek Poetry* (London: Routledge, 1990); John Hollander, *The Figure of Echo: A Mode of Allusion in Milton and After* (Berkeley and Los

Angeles: University of California Press, 1981); William Porter, *Reading the Classics and "Paradise Lost"* (Lincoln: University of Nebraska Press, 1993); Allan Pasco, *Allusion: A Literary Graft* (Toronto: University of Toronto Press, 1994); John Hale, "Milton Playing with Ovid," *Milton Studies*, vol. 25, ed. James D. Simmonds (Pittsburgh: University of Pittsburgh Press, 1989), 3–19. Christopher Ricks, *Allusion to the Poets* (New York: Oxford University Press, 2002), invents a new metaphor to describe the workings of almost every allusion he examines.

5. Jane Melbourne, "Biblical Intertextuality in *Samson Agonistes*," *SEL* 36 (Winter 1996): 111–27; Anne Lake Prescott, "Intertextual Topology: English Writers and Pantagruel's Hell," *English Literary Renaissance* 23 (Spring 1993): 244–66.

6. Julia Kristeva, "The Bounded Text," trans. Thomas Gora, Alice Jardine, and Leon S. Roudiez, in *Desire in Language: A Semiotic Approach to Literature and Art*, ed. Leon S. Roudiez (New York: Columbia University Press, 1980), 36–63, esp. 37–38.

7. Culler, "Presupposition and Intertextuality," 100, 109, 103; emphasis mine.

8. Julia Kristeva, *Revolution in Poetic Language*, trans. Margaret Waller (New York: Columbia University Press, 1984), 60.

9. Ibid., 60.

10. Kristeva, "The Bounded Text," 36, and "Word, Dialogue and Novel," trans. Thomas Gora, Alice Jardine, and Leon S. Roudiez, in *Desire in Language: A Semiotic Approach to Literature and Art*, ed. Leon S. Roudiez, 64–91 (New York: Columbia University Press, 1980), 65, 66.

11. Kristeva, "The Bounded Text," 38.

12. Ibid., 41.

13. Ibid., 42, 44–45.

14. Culler, "Presupposition and Intertextuality," 109, 103; emphasis mine.

15. James Hodder, *Hoders Decimall Arithmatick* (London, 1667), i.

16. Ibid., iii–iv.

17. Kristeva, "The Bounded Text," 38–39.

18. Ibid., 39–40.

19. Louis Montrose, "Professing the Renaissance: The Poetics and Politics of Culture," in *The New Historicism*, ed. H. Aram Veeser (New York: Routledge, 1989), 17.

20. Robert Alter, *The Pleasures of Reading in an Ideological Age* (New York: Simon and Schuster, 1989), draws the distinction between allusion in the sense of verbal echo and of learned or roundabout reference, but then almost immediately confuses the issue again by naming the former "literary allusion," an inadequately distinguishing term, since both occur *in* literary texts and either sort could be *to* a literary text.

21. Dictionaries of allusion, incidentally, themselves point up the difference between the two phenomena conflated under the name *allusion*, for they are always dictionaries of learned references; a dictionary of phraseological adaptation could not exist because it would have to reproduce the entire literary canon. Not even a source like Bartlett's *Familiar Quotations* can serve as a reference work for verbal echoes, since poets do not always allude to the famous, pithy statements that comprise such compilations.

22. Charlotte Smith, *The Poems of Charlotte Smith*, ed. Stuart Curran (New York: Oxford University Press, 1993), 71, line 3.

23. A. E. Housman, "Terence, this is stupid stuff," in *Collected Poems and Selected Prose of A. E. Housman*, ed. Christopher Ricks (London: Allen Lane, 1988).

24. This is especially true when one considers the many phraseolgical adaptations of texts originally written in a different language than the alluding text, where part of what is involved in the appropriation is translation.

25. John K. Hale, "The Classical Literary Tradition," in *A Companion to Milton*, ed. Thomas N. Corns, 22–36 (Oxford: Blackwell, 2001), 26.

26. I. A. Richards, *The Philosophy of Rhetoric* (New York: Oxford University Press, 1936), 96.

27. Ziva Ben-Porat, "The Poetics of Literary Allusion," *PTL: A Journal for Descriptive Poetics and Theory of Literature* 1 (1976): 107; emphasis mine. Garner, *From Homer to Tragedy*, 6.

28. Ben-Porat, "Poetics of Literary Allusion," 112.

29. Porter, *Reading the Classics*, 30.

30. Edward Stein, *Wordsworth's Art of Allusion* (University Park: Pennsylvania State University Press, 1988), 223, 3.

31. Porter, *Reading the Classics*, 17–35.

32. James Scudamore, *Homer à la Mode* (London, 1665).

33. Ibid., 3, 72, 31, 112.

34. Ibid., 43, 60.

35. Barbara Herrnstein Smith, "Contingencies of Value," *Critical Inquiry* 10 (September 1983): 5–39, esp. 27–35. John Guillory, "Canon," in *Critical Terms for Literary Study*, ed. Frank Lentricchia and Thomas McLaughlin (Chicago: University of Chicago Press, 1990), 233–49, esp. 237.

36. Smith, "Contingencies of Value," 34–35.

37. David Norbrook, *Writing the Republic: Poetry, Rhetoric and Politics, 1627–1660* (Cambridge: Cambridge University Press, 1999), 438–67.

38. In addition to Norbrook, Rachel Falconer, *Orpheus Dis(re)membered: Milton and the Myth of the Poet Hero* (Sheffield: Sheffield Academic Press, 1996), 24–38, examines Milton's treatment of the figure of Orpheus as portrayed in Virgil and Ovid, and considers contrasting

treatments of the myth by Milton's contemporaries, showing, for example, how the legendary singer could be appropriated to support either royalist or Republican views on the limits of monarchial authority.

39. *Aeneid* 12.950. Citations from the *Aeneid* are from the translation of Allan Mandlebaum (New York: Bantam, 1971), hereafter cited in the text by book and line number. The Latin original is quoted from the edition of R. D. Williams, 2 vols. (Basingstoke: Macmillan, 1972).

40. Virgil, *Opera*, ed. Charles de La Rue (London, 1687), 173.

41. Samuel Monk, *The Sublime: A Study of Critical Theories in Eighteenth-Century England* (Ann Arbor, Mich.: Ann Arbor Paperbacks, 1960), 29.

42. Rene Rapin, *Observations on the Poems of Homer and Virgil*, trans. John Davies (London, 1672), 91–92, 93.

43. John Dryden, *The Works of John Dryden*, vol. 5, ed. Alan Roper (Berkeley and Los Angeles: University of California Press, 1987), 286, 315–18.

44. Charles de Saint-Evremond, *Miscellaneous Essays by Monsieur St. Euremont* (London, 1692), 180.

45. Patrick Hume, *Annotations on Milton's "Paradise Lost"* (London, 1695), 188.

46. John Milton, *Paradise Lost*, ed. Thomas Newton (London, 1749), 362.

47. John Henry Todd, ed., *The Poetical Work of John Milton*, 4 vols. (London: Rivingtons, 1842).

48. John Milton, *Complete Poems and Major Prose*, ed. Merritt Y. Hughes (New York: Macmillan, 1957); John Milton, *Paradise Lost*, ed. Alastair Fowler (London: Longman, 1968), 298.

49. Fowler, *Paradise Lost*, 101.

50. Roy Flannagan, ed., *The Riverside Milton* (Boston: Houghton Mifflin, 1998), 496.

51. Hume, *Annotations*, 3.

52. *PL* 2.439; Hume, *Annotations*, 67.

53. Howard Clarke, *Homer's Readers: A Historical Introduction to the "Iliad" and the "Odyssey"* (Newark: University of Delaware Press, 1981), 97.

54. Alexander Pope, *Poetry and Prose of Alexander Pope*, ed. Aubrey Williams (New York: Houghton Mifflin, 1969), 134–35.

55. Clarke, *Homer's Readers*, characterizes twentieth century critics' focus as being on such larger-scale matters, demonstrating "what many readers intuit, that [the poems] are indeed well-made stories" (282).

56. Flannagan, *Riverside Milton*, 297, 298.

57. I want to make clear that I am not seeking to correct an oversight by Hughes, Fowler, or Flannagan, or to impugn their classical scholarship. In my argument, it cannot be otherwise. Given the way in which

our culture presently constructs Homer, his status as the source for Milton's phrase "ambrosial night" is largely inconsequential.

58. Plutarch, *Essay on the Life and Poetry of Homer*, ed. J. J. Keaney and Robert Lamberton (Atlanta: Scholars Press, 1996), 215.

59. Ibid., 1.

Notes to Chapter 2

1. Stella Purce Revard, *The War in Heaven: "Paradise Lost" and the Tradition of Satan's Rebellion* (Ithaca: Cornell University Press, 1980), uses the term *exemplum* occasionally in her comprehensive overview of the theological and poetic traditions that inform the episode, but only in passing (48, 287). In her conclusion, she provides a rich consideration of what Eve and Adam *might* each have drawn from Raphael's narrative in facing their own temptations, how it *ought* to have functioned as an exemplum (278–81).

2. Joseph Addison, *Critical Essays from "The Spectator,"* ed. Donald F. Bond (New York: Oxford University Press, 1970), 74; Samuel Johnson, *The Lives of the Most Eminent English Poets* (Oxford: Clarendon Press, 2006), 290.

3. Arnold Stein, *Answerable Style: Essays on "Paradise Lost"* (Minneapolis: University of Minnesota Press, 1953), 20.

4. David Farley-Hills *The Benevolence of Laughter: Comic Poetry of the Commonwealth and Restoration* (Totowa, N.J.: Rowman and Littlefield, 1974), 119–20.

5. Isabel G. MacCaffrey, *"Paradise Lost": Books 5 and 6*, ed. Robert Hodge and Isabel G. MacCaffrey (Cambridge: Cambridge University Press, 1975); Barbara Kiefer Lewalski, *"Paradise Lost" and the Rhetoric of Literary Forms* (Princeton, N.J.: Princeton University Press, 1985), 332; David Quint, *Epic and Empire: Politics and Generic Form from Virgil to Milton* (Princeton, N.J.: Princeton University Press, 1993), 47–48. Revard, while recognizing the importance of generic issues, declines an explicit generic classification: "If we approach the war in Heaven, therefore, knowing and responding to the political, religious, and poetical traditions Milton was aware of, we may come to understand it not just, as the eighteenth century urged, as a fine piece of Homeric imitation, or as the mid-twentieth century exhorted, as a mock epic within epic, but as a finely wrought episode in its own right that reflects many traditions and lends manifold meaning to the whole of *Paradise Lost*" (27).

6. James Wooton, "The Poet's War: Violence and Virtue in *Paradise Lost*," *SEL* 30 (Winter 1990): 142.

7. In the opening of his *Heroic Mockery* (Newark, Del.: University of Delaware Press, 1977), George de Forest Lord calls attention to this distinction; the very phrase *heroic mockery* is coined to permit discussion of those poems that ridicule the heroic codes celebrated in ancient epic.

8. Surprisingly, in Charles Martindale's *John Milton and the Transformation of Ancient Epic* (Totowa, N.J.: Barnes & Noble, 1986), which proposes to provide direct scrutiny of Milton's relation to Homer, book 6 is scarcely examined.

9. Lord, *Heroic Mockery*, 67.

10. This technique of using Homer against himself has also been discussed by Martindale, *Milton and the Transformation*, 75–76.

11. *PL* 5.600, *Iliad* 8.5; *PL* 5.647, *Iliad* 2.1; *PL* 6.245, *Iliad* 12.433; *PL* 6.819–21, *Iliad* 8.18–27; *PL* 6.832, *Iliad* 1.47; *PL* 6.838, *Iliad* 15.322.

12. Edmund Spenser, *The Faerie Queene: Book One*, ed. Carol V. Kaske (Indianapolis: Hackett, 2006), 205–06.

13. Torquato Tasso, *Discourse on the Heroic Poem*, trans. Mariella Gavalchini and Irene Samuel (Oxford: Clarendon Press, 1973), 10.

14. Sir Philip Sidney, *The Prose Works of Sir Philip Sidney*, 4 vols., ed. Albert Feuillerat (Cambridge: Cambridge University Press, 1962), 3:11, 14.

15. Spenser, *Faerie Queene*, 205.

16. Ibid., 205–06; emphasis added.

17. J. A. Mosher, *Exemplum in the Early Religious and Didactic Literature of England* (New York: Columbia University Press, 1911), 8.

18. For a more detailed reading of the episode, see chapter 3 of Margaret Olofson Thickstun, *Milton's "Paradise Lost": Moral Education* (New York: Palgrave Macmillan, 2007). She reads the episode in terms of the social psychology of group dynamics but with a strong focus on the moral decision making depicted in it.

19. See Brian S. Lee, "'This is No Fable': Historical Residues in Two Medieval Exempla," *Speculum: A Journal of Medieval Studies* 56 (October 1981): 728–66.

20. Jeffrey Lyons, *Exemplum: The Rhetoric of Example in Early Modern France and Italy* (Princeton, N.J.: Princeton University Press, 1990), 27.

21. For the predominance of admonitory exempla, see G. R. Owst, *Literature and Pulpit in Medieval England* (New York: Barnes & Noble, 1961), 161.

22. For the range of imitative approaches that Renaissance theory held a later author might take toward a precursor, see G. W. Pigman, "Versions of Imitation in the Renaissance," *Renaissance Quarterly* 33 (1980): 1–32.

23. Harold Bloom, *A Map of Misreading* (Oxford: Oxford University Press, 1975), esp. 125–43.

24. John Steadman, *Milton and the Renaissance Hero* (Oxford: Clarendon Press, 1967), 174, in an argument that will be explored in greater detail in the following chapter, claims that an allusion like this "exposes the heroic pretences of [Homer's] traditional heroes as essentially diabolical."

Notes to Chapter 3

1. Thomas Greene, *The Descent from Heaven: A Study in Epic Continuity* (New Haven: Yale University Press, 1963), 3.

2. Judith Kates, *Tasso and Milton* (Lewisburg, PA: Bucknell University Press, 1983).

3. Gambara is cited from Bernard Weinburg's *History of Literary Criticism in the Italian Renaissance* (Chicago: University of Chicago Press, 1961), 306–08. Andrew Marvell's prefatory poem "On *Paradise Lost*" expresses the fear he had while reading the epic that Milton would "ruine (for I saw him strong) / The sacred Truths to Fable and old Song" (CM 2.1.3) Among modern critics, Ernst Robert Curtius, *European Literature and the Latin Middle Ages*, trans. Willard R. Trask (London: Routledge & Kegan Paul, 1953), 462, calls the Christian epic a *genre faux*; Northrop Frye, *Five Essays on Milton's Epics* (London: Routledge & Kegan Paul, 1966), 5, calls it a "huge, impossible ideal." For John Steadman, *Milton and the Paradoxes of Renaissance Heroism* (Baton Rouge: Louisana State University Press, 1987), 7, writing a Christian epic is the poetic equivalent of squaring a circle. Thomas Greene (*Descent from Heaven*, 3) deems the desire of Renaissance authors to compose a Christian epic "delusory."

4. Greene, *Descent from Heaven*, 3.

5. John Steadman, *Milton and the Renaissance Hero* (Oxford: Clarendon Press, 1967), 170, 174.

6. Ibid., 17; Kates, *Tasso and Milton*, 68.

7. Francis C. Blessington, *"Paradise Lost" and the Classical Epic* (Boston: Routledge and Kegan Paul, 1979).

8. Martin Mueller, "Homer," in *A Milton Encyclopedia*, 9 vols., ed. William B. Hunter et al. (Lewisburg, Pa.: Bucknell University Press, 1978–83), 4:13; emphasis added.

9. Torquato Tasso, *Discourses on the Heroic Poem*, trans. Mariella Gavalchini and Irene Samuel (Oxford: Clarendon Press, 1973), 16; emphasis added.

10. Torquato Tasso, *Jerusalem Delivered*, trans. Ralph Nash (Detroit: Wayne State University Press, 1987), canto 8, stanza 2; hereafter cited as *JD*, followed by canto and stanza number.

11. *Iliad* 1.477, 24.788; *Odyssey* 2.1, 3.404, 3.491, 4.306, 4.431, 4.576, 5.228, 8.1, 9.152, 9.170, 9.307, 9.437, 9.560, 10.187, 12.8, 12.316, 13.18, 15.189, 17.1, 19.428.

12. *Iliad* 3.373, 5.311, 8.91, 17.530, 18.165, 23.154; *Odyssey* 16.220, 21.226.

13. William Porter, *Reading the Classics and "Paradise Lost"* (Lincoln: University of Nebraska Press, 1993), 20.

14. In chapter 3 of *Milton among the Romans: The Pedagogy and Influence of Milton's Curriculum* (Pittsburgh: Duquesne University Press, 2001), Richard J. DuRocher considers this passage in connection

with Vitruvius's *De architectura*. Perhaps, in the context of a description informed by classical architectural theory (and in conjunction with the preceding simile of an organ breathing a blast of wind through a sound-board), the reference to "exhalation" might be read as suggesting that the foundation of Pandaemonium is less solid even than sand—mere air. But even were that so, it would be the word *exhalation* that carries that meaning; the reference to Thetis's emergence from the sea has little significant resonance in the immediate context of Milton's reprise of the Homeric line.

15. John T. Shawcross, *With Mortal Voice: The Creation of "Paradise Lost"* (Lexington: University Press of Kentucky, 1982), 77, quotes from Pope's translation ("And as on corn when western gusts descend, / Before the blast the lofty harvests bend: / Thus o'er the field the moving host appears, / With nodding ploumes and groves of waving spears"). This gives the impression that it is Homer who mentions the spears, when in fact it is Milton who adds that detail to the vehicle of the metaphor. (Indeed, it is likely that Pope imports the spears into Homer's metaphor from Milton.)

16. Ibid., 77.

17. Ibid., 77.

18. Charles Martindale, *John Milton and the Transformation of Ancient Epic* (Totowa, N.J.: Barnes & Noble, 1986), 13.

19. Martin Mueller, "The Tragic Epic: *Paradise Lost* and the *Iliad*" (Ph.D. diss., Indiana University, Bloomington, 1966), 60, 75; David Masson, *The Poetical Works of John Milton*, 3 vols. (London: Macmillan, 1890), 1:56; Martindale, *Transformation*, 13; Porter, *Reading the Classics*, 94

20. Martindale, *Transformation*, 14.

21. *PL* 2.43; *Iliad* 1.279, 2.86; *Odyssey* 2.231, 4.64, 5.9, 8.41.

22. *Iliad* 3.95, 7.92, 7.398, 8.28, 9.29, 9.430, 9.689, 10.218, 10.313, 23.676; *Odyssey* 8.234, 11.33, 13.1, 16.393, 20.320.

23. *Iliad* 1.148, 2.245, 4.349, 4.411, 5.251, 5.888, 10.446, 12.230, 14.82, 15.13, 17.141, 17.169, 18.284, 20.428, 22.260, 22.344, 24.559; *Odyssey* 8.165, 17.459, 18.14, 18.337, 18.388, 19.70, 22.34, 22.320.

24. There is one situation in which Milton's alluding to a Homeric stock phrase causes no difficulty in assigning a significance to the allusion. This is true when, as is often the case, the Homeric formula is consistently used in a similar context. For example, before the exchange of blows between Abdiel and Satan, Milton has Abdiel offer the taunt "fool, not to think how vain / Against th' Omnipotent to rise in Arms" (6.135–36). There are four moments in the *Iliad* when Homer uses the word *fool* (νήπιος) in the vocative case, as Abdiel does here, but each of them occurs in roughly the same context. Each time a Homeric hero vaunts with the term *fool*, it is in a situation where his opponent is clearly doomed. If we assume that Milton is appropriating this resonance, then a reader of *Paradise Lost* who

remembers Homer's customary use of the vocative νηπιε, a reader, in fact, who remembers any one of the Homeric passages, realizes that Satan's rebellion is doomed from the outset. Homer's formulaic diction, though it must be kept ever in mind, need not in all cases make it impossible to assign a meaning to one of Milton's allusions.

25. Milman Parry, *The Collected Works of Milman Parry*, ed. Adam Parry (Oxford: Clarendon Press, 1971), 139–40.

26. Albert B. Lord, *The Singer of Tales* (Cambridge, Mass.: Harvard University Press, 1960), 142–44.

27. Masson, *Poetical Works of Milton*, 56.

28. Kates, *Tasso and Milton*, 55.

Notes to Chapter 4

1. John Dennis, *The Grounds of Criticism in Poetry* (London, 1704), b2v.

2. Samuel Johnson, *The Lives of the Most Eminent English Poets*, ed. Roger Lonsdale (Oxford: Clarendon Press, 2006), 294.

3. Ibid., 295.

4. Barbara Lewalski, *The Life of John Milton* (Oxford: Blackwell, 2000), 46.

5. Roland Mortier, *L'originalité, une nouvelle catégorie esthétique au siècle des lumières* (Geneva: Droz, 1982), 31, traces a similar development in the French language.

6. The nominalized form, *originality*, represents an even later semantic development; the *OED*'s earliest witness is from 1787.

7. David Quint, *Origin and Originality in Renaissance Literature* (New Haven: Yale University Press, 1983); see especially his treatment of Jean Chapelain, whom he considers in conjunction with Milton (214–20).

8. Regina Schwartz, *Remembering and Repeating: Biblical Creation in "Paradise Lost"* (Cambridge: Cambridge University Press, 1988), 1.

9. In Schwartz's formulation, for Milton, "the original act is an iteration" (ibid., 1).

10. Giulio Cesare Scaliger, *Poetices libri septem* (Lyon, 1561), 214; translation mine.

11. Edmund Spenser, *The Faerie Queene: Book One*, ed. Carol V. Kaske (Indianapolis: Hackett, 2006), 205. Scaliger, *Poetices libri septem*, 215: "Homerus ergo com vitae nostrae duas instituerit rationes, civilem prudentiam in Ulyssea, militarem in Iliade, easque tanquam duas species in duobus viris ostendisset, in uno utranque Aenea composuit Maro, cui etiam sicut alibi diximus, addiderit pietatem" [Homer teaches the two principles of our lives, civil prudence in the *Odyssey* and military in the *Iliad*. He exhibits them in two men, whereas Virgil composed them in

the single figure of Aeneas, and as we said in another place, added the quality of piety as well].

12. George Chapman, *Chapman's Homer: The Iliad*, ed. Allardyce Nicoll (Princeton, N.J.: Princeton University Press, 1984), 14.

13. In John Ogilby's 1660 translation, Paterculus's quote also receives special emphasis. In a prefatory section of encomia to Homer, after a set of verse tributes, the Paterculus quote is one of just two prose passages cited (the other is by Quintillian). In James Duport's exactly contemporaneous *Homeri gnomologia*, fully 238 testimonials are cited. That Ogilby should choose, from such a large potential corpus, just the Paterculus quote suggests that its focus on Homer's originality was felt to have a special force at this historical moment.

14. James Duport, *Homeri gnomologia* (London, 1660), xiii.

15. Lodovico Castelvetro, *Castelvetro on the Art of Poetry*, trans. Andrew Bongiorno (Binghamton, N.Y.: Medieval & Renaissance Texts & Studies, 1984), 105.

16. Giulo Cesare Scaliger, *Select Translations from Scaliger's Poetics*, trans. Frederick Morgan Padelford (New York: H. Holt, 1905), 75.

17. Ibid., 77; emphasis mine.

18. T. S. Eliot, *Selected Prose of T. S. Eliot*, ed. Frank Kermode (New York: Harcourt, Brace Jovanovich, 1975), 38.

19. Harold Bloom, *The Anxiety of Influence* (Oxford: Oxford University Press, 1973), 7; hereafter cited parenthetically in the text as *Anxiety*.

20. Harold Bloom, *The Western Canon* (New York: Harcourt Brace, 1994), 29; hereafter cited parenthetically in the text as *Canon*.

21. Harold Bloom, *A Map of Misreading* (Oxford: Oxford University Press, 1975), 77; hereafter cited parenthetically in the text as *Map*.

22. Robert Moynihan, "Interview: Harold Bloom," *Diacritics* 13 (1983): 57–68. Though he has treated Milton since that interview, in both *Ruin the Sacred Truths* and *The Western Canon*, it is not clear whether Bloom has yet developed what he would regard as an adequate account. Robert Adams, "Bloom's All-Time Greatest Hits," *The New York Review of Books*, Nov. 17, 1994, 6, regards Bloom's chapter on *Paradise Lost* in *The Western Canon* as one of the weakest readings in that book.

23. Thomas Carew, "An Elegy upon the Death of Dr. Donne, Dean of Pauls," *Poems of Thomas Carew* (London: Routledge & Sons, 1899), 101, line 28.

24. Harold Bloom, *Agon: Towards a Theory of Revisionism* (Oxford: Oxford University Press), 21.

25. Bloom, *Map of Misreading*, 130, citing a passage from Samuel Johnson's "Life of Milton," *Lives of the Most Eminent English Poets*, 287.

26. *Iliad* 19. 373–74; *Faerie Queene* 5.5.3.

27. Johnson, *Lives of the Most Eminent English Poets*, 287.

28. In the critical response to Bloom's work, nobody elects to study his texts as poems. Bloom, *Kabbalah and Criticism* (New York: Seabury Press, 1975), 109, insists that "a theory of poetry must itself be poetry" and speaks of his theory as one that "presents itself as a severe poem" (*Anxiety* 13). But even critics sympathetic with his project—such as Peter DeBolla, *Harold Bloom: Towards Historical Rhetorics* (London: Routledge, 1988); Jean-Pierre Mileur, *Literary Revisionism and the Burden of Modernity* (Berkeley and Los Angeles: University of California Press, 1985); and David Fite, *Harold Bloom: The Rhetoric of Romantic Vision* (Amherst: University of Massachusetts Press, 1985)—value Bloom's texts as arguments rather than explicating them as poems. Daniel O'Hara, "The Genius of Irony: Nietzsche in Bloom," in *The Yale Critics: Deconstruction in America,* ed. Jonathan Arac, Wlad Godzich, and Wallace Martin, 111–29 (Minneapolis: University of Minnesota Press, 1983), demonstrates that Bloom's appropriations of Nietzsche can be described using Bloom's own revisionary ratios.

29. That it serves at least some readers as a plausible account of Milton's poetic practice is evident from the way Bloom's once radical reading of *Paradise Lost* has entered mainstream Milton criticism. Quint, *Origin and Originality,* for example, adopts Bloom's sense that Milton "reverses the relationship between *Paradise Lost* and the tradition of earlier texts which it imitates" (213). And even though Barbara Lewalski, *"Paradise Lost" and the Rhetoric of Literary Forms* (Princeton, N.J.: Princeton University Press, 1985), rejects his approach—"though I focus upon Milton's engagement with literary precursors I do not find that engagement characterized by anxiety, struggle, transumption or triumph"—her footnote presents Bloom's view as at least potentially valid, calmly directing readers, "for the counter argument, see Harold Bloom, *A Map of Misreading"* (39).

30. Nicolas Boileau, *Oeuvres complètes* ([Paris]: Gallimard, 1979), 518–19.

31. The introduction to Richmond Lattimore's translation of the *Iliad* shows how details in Homer's extended similes often have no referent in the object from the war at Troy that occasioned them, but instead take readers temporarily to the more familiar world of peacetime agricultural labor (40–43). By contrast, Viktor Pöschl's *The Art of Virgil: Image and Symbol in the Aeneid,* trans. Gerda Seligson (Ann Arbor: University of Michigan Press, 1962) carefully exhibits the ways in which all details from the tenor of Virgil's extended similes generally bear in some subtle way on aspects of the tenor. In *Milton among the Romans: The Pedagogy and Influence of Milton's Latin Curriculum* (Pittsburgh: Duquesne University Press, 2001), Richard J. DuRocher offers a salutary reading of the ploughman in Milton's famous simile (4.977–85) as having neither God nor Satan as its tenor; the ploughman is just a ploughman, an ele-

ment in the vehicle of the extended simile that corresponds to nothing in the tenor (69). The same principle governing the operation of long-tailed similes might be invoked to counter the "logical inference" that drives John Leonard's reading of the ploughman simile in his "Milton's Careful Ploughman: An Impossible Simile," in *Milton, Rights and Liberties,* ed. Christophe Tournu and Neil Forsyth (Bern: Peter Lang, 2007); because the ears of grain in the vehicle are threatened does not, in the context of an epic simile, necessarily imply that the good angel's spears in the tenor are similarly threatened; they are only what the poet says: "as thick" as grain that is in a certain meteorological circumstance (then the nature of such grain is captured richly in its own right).

32. Raymond Williams, *Keywords: A Vocabulary of Culture and Society* (New York: Oxford University Press, 1976), 192–93, notes the variety of perspectives from which origins and originality can be viewed and gives some sense of the historical shift I have isolated for consideration.

33. The binary character of Milton's imagination is of increasing interest to Miltonists. See, for instance, Sanford Budick, *The Dividing Muse: Images of Sacred Disjunction in Milton's Poetry* (New Haven: Yale University Press, 1985); Gordon Teskey, "From Allegory to Dialectic: Imagining Error in Spenser and Milton" *PMLA* 101 (1986): 9–23; and especially R. A. Shoaf, *Milton, Poet of Duality* (New Haven: Yale University Press, 1985). Regina Schwartz, *Remembering and Repeating: Biblical Creation in "Paradise Lost"* (Cambridge: Cambridge University Press, 1988), addresses, though in terms different from mine, Milton's binary conception of origins.

34. Quint, *Origin and Originality,* 213.

35. Ibid., 216.

36. Ibid., 214.

Notes to Chapter 5

1. John Dryden, "Lines on Milton," in *The Works of John Dryden,* ed. H. T. Swedenberg (Berkeley and Los Angeles: University of California Press, 1969), 3:208; Joseph Addison, *Critical Essays from "The Spectator,"* ed. Donald F. Bond (New York: Oxford University Press, 1970), 72; Samuel Johnson, *The Lives of the Most Eminent English Poets* (Oxford: Clarendon Press, 2006), 286.

2. Samuel Monk, *The Sublime: A Study of Critical Theories in Eighteenth-Century England* (Ann Arbor, Mich.: Ann Arbor Paperbacks, 1960), 20.

3. Ibid., 20.

4. Annabel Patterson, *Reading between the Lines* (London: Routledge, 1993), 258. David Norbrook, *Writing the English Republic:*

Poetry, Rhetoric and Politics, 1627–1660 (Cambridge: Cambridge University Press, 1999), also finds the Longinian sublime an operative concept in England well before Boileau.

5. Jules Brody, *Boileau and Longinus* (Geneva: Droz, 1958), 9–18.

6. Ibid., 88, 13.

7. Longinus, *On the Sublime*, trans. W. H. Fyfe, rev. Donald Russell, in *Aristotle*, vol. 23 (Cambridge, Mass.: Harvard University Press, 1995), vii, xi.

8. Brody, *Boileau and Longinus*, 91. This association of simplicity with sublimity represents, as Brody points out, a significant theoretical development; for classical rhetoric, simplicity was associated with the lowest of the three discursive registers: the *genus humile* or *submissum*.

9. Francesco Petrarch, *Rerum familiarium libri I–VII*, trans. Aldo S. Bernardo (Albany, N.Y.: State University of New York Press, 1975), 46.

10. Quintilian, *Institutiones oratoriae* (Cambridge, Mass.: Harvard University Press, 2001), 10.2.9–10.

11. Erasmus, *The Collected Works of Erasmus: Literary and Educational Writings 6, Ciceronianus*, ed. A. H. T Levi (Toronto: University of Toronto Press, 1986), 28:446. See also G. W. Pigman, "Versions of Imitation in the Renaissance," *Renaissance Quarterly* 33, no. 1 (1980): 1–32.

12. Charles Martindale, *John Milton and the Transformation of Ancient Epic* (Totowa, N.J.: Barnes & Noble, 1986), 80.

13. Hesiod, "Theogony," in *Hesiod, the Homeric Hymns and Homerica*, trans. Hugh G. Evelyn-White (Cambridge, Mass.: Harvard University Press, 1982), line 720.

14. Edward Philips, "Compendiosa enumeratio poetarum," in John Buchler, *Sacrarum prophanarumque phrasium poeticarum thesaurus*, 17th ed. (London, 1669), 399, quoted in Barbara Lewalski, *The Life of John Milton* (Oxford: Blackwell, 2000), 492.

15. Jonathan Richardson, "Explanatory Notes and Remarks," in *Early Lives of Milton*, ed. Helen Darbishire (London: Constable, 1932), 296.

16. Brody, *Boileau and Longinus*, 113–17.

17. John Ogilby, *Homer His Iliads Translated* (London, 1660), 390.

18. Kirsti Simonsuuri, *Homer's Original Genius: Eighteenth-Century Notions of the Early Greek Epic (1688–1798)* (Cambridge: Cambridge University Press), 9, 11.

19. Ibid., 13, 12–13.

20. James Duport, *Homeri gnomologia* (London, 1660), vi.

21. Johannes Ravisius Textor [Jean Tixier de Ravise], *Epithetorum* (Basel, 1635).

22. Meric Casaubon, *Treatise concerning Enthusiasm* (London, 1654), 174, 203–04.

Notes to Chapter 6

1. Allan H. Gilbert, *On the Composition of "Paradise Lost"* (Chapel Hill: University of North Carolina Press, 1947), offers an elaborate account of *how* Milton may have gone about converting a drama on the Fall ("perhaps wholly written") into the epic we now have, but he leaves unconsidered the question of *why* Milton decided to make that change in genre (23).

2. John Guillory, "Canon," in *Critical Terms for Literary Study,* ed. Frank Lentricchia and Thomas McLaughlin (Chicago: University of Chicago Press, 1990), 237.

3. Throughout his book, John Guillory, *Cultural Capital: The Problem of Literary Canon Formation* (Chicago: University of Chicago Press, 1993), criticizes the contemporary project of making the canon "representative," but his alternative (universalizing access to the evaluation of literature) is not satisfying even to himself; he undercuts the proposal by labeling it a mere "thought experiment" (340).

4. This possibility is mentioned by Regina Schwartz, *Remembering and Repeating: Biblical Creation in "Paradise Lost"* (Cambridge: Cambridge University Press, 1988), 88.

5. As Mary Ann Radzinowicz, *Toward "Samson Agonistes": The Growth of Milton's Mind* (Princeton, N.J.: Princeton University Press, 1978), argues, "he believed in a purified and elevated stage, not in the existing commercial stage. He planned to write for a reformed theater" (396).

6. Harris Francis Fletcher, ed., *John Milton's Complete Poetical Works Reproduced in Photographic Facsimile,* 4 vols. (Urbana: University of Illinois Press, 1945), 16–18.

7. *The Complete Prose Works of John Milton,* 8 vols., ed. Don M. Wolfe et al. (New Haven: Yale University Press, 1953–82), 8:555, 557.

8. The translations are those from John Milton, *Complete Poetry and Major Prose,* ed. Merritt Y. Hughes (New York: Macmillan, 1957).

9. E. M. W. Tillyard, *Milton* (London: Chatto and Windus, 1930), too, regards *Areopagitica* as a "transitional" document in Milton's growing disillusion with the parliamentary government, followed not long after by the explicitly pessimistic sonnet "I did but prompt the age" (199).

10. A small error by Milton's student and biographer Edward Phillips provides further evidence that Milton was experimenting with his school to determine whether such a setting might ensure the perpetuation of his work. In his biography Phillips quotes the ten lines presently at 4.32–41 of *Paradise Lost,* revealing they were initially "designed for the very beginning of [a] tragedy." In the final line of his citation, Phillips has "Warring in Heaven, against Heaven's glorious king," whereas in the epic the line reads "Warring in Heaven, against Heaven's matchless king."

Perhaps as a student Phillips had memorized the lines as they appear in his biography. Years later, when the epic actually appeared, Phillips might, on recognizing the passage that he had memorized as a youngster, have skimmed through it without noting Milton's single alteration. And later still, when he composed his biography, he might have reproduced the passage from memory, without consulting the text of *Paradise Lost*. I read Phillips misquotation, in other words, as evidence that—at the very time that the possibility of writing for a reformed, state-sponsored theater evaporated—Milton was using his small school as a testing ground to determine whether academic institutions might serve to perpetuate his planned literary works.

11. In the preface to the printed play, Davenant apologizes that in the initial performance the scenery could not be as elaborate as it should have been because the ceiling of Rutland House was only 11 feet high, but the existing sketches by John Webb suggest that, despite these lamentable constraints, the sets were quite elaborate. See Leslie Hotson, *The Commonwealth and Restoration Stage* (Cambridge, Mass.: Harvard University Press, 1926), 154.

12. Abraham Cowley, *Poems* (London, 1656), preface.

13. Jean Loiseau, *Abraham Cowley's Reputation in England* (Paris, 1931), 3.

14. Quoted in ibid., 10.

15. Ibid., 7.

16. Stanley Fish, *Surprised by Sin: The Reader in "Paradise Lost"* (Berkeley and Los Angeles: University of California Press, 1967); Radzinowicz, *Toward "Samson Agonistes"*; Ann Baynes Coiro, "'To Repair the Ruins of Our First Parents': Education and the Fallen Adam," *Studies in English Literature* 28 (Winter 1988): 133–47; Anna K. Nardo, "Academic Interludes in *Paradise Lost*," in *Milton Studies* 27 (1991): 209–41; Barbara K. Lewalski, "Milton and the Hartlib Circle: Educational Projects and Epic Paideia," in *Literary Milton: Text, Pretext, Context*, ed. Diana Treviño Benet and Michael Lieb (Pittsburgh: Duquesne University Press, 1994); Richard J. DuRocher, *Milton among the Romans: The Pedagogy and Influence of Milton's Latin Curriculum* (Pittsburgh: Duquesne University Press, 2001); Margaret Olofson Thickstun, *Milton's "Paradise Lost": Moral Education* (New York: Palgrave Macmillan, 2007).

17. James Bowen, *A History of Western Education* (New York: St. Martins, 1972), 3:104.

18. Johann Amos Comenius, *The Orbis Pictus of John Amos Comenius*, trans. Charles Hoole (Syracuse, N.Y.: C. W. Bardeen, 1887), 37–38; hereafter cited in the text as *Orbis*.

19. Thickstun, *Milton's "Paradise Lost,"* stops short of claiming that the epic was written *for* college-age readers, but elaborates how well

suited its material is for students at that stage in their development of moral reasoning, arguing that the epic "addresses directly the issues of self-determination and personal responsibility that [college sophomores] face in their lives" (1).

Notes to the Conclusion

1. Barbara Herrnstein Smith, "Contingencies of Value," *Critical Inquiry* 10 (Sept. 1983): 5–39, 27–28.

2. Ibid., 30.

3. Terry Eagleton. *Literary Theory: An Introduction.* 2nd ed. (Minneapolis: University of Minnesota Press, 1996), 10.

4. Michel Foucault, *The Order of Things: An Archaeology of the Human Sciences* (New York: Random House, 1970), xi–xii.

5. Daniel Javitch, *Proclaiming a Classic: The Canonization of "Orlando Furioso"* (Princeton, N.J.: Princeton University Press, 1991); Gary Taylor, *Reinventing Shakespeare: A Cultural History from the Restoration to the Present* (New York: Weidenfield and Nicholson, 1989).

6. Stephen Fallon, *Milton's Peculiar Grace: Self-Representation and Authority* (Ithaca: Cornell University Press, 2007), 173.

7. Sir Philip Sidney, *The Prose Works of Sir Philip Sidney*, 4 vols., ed. Albert Feuillerat (Cambridge: Cambridge University Press, 1912–26), 3:11.

8. Joseph Addison, *Critical Essays from the "Spectator,"* ed. Donald F. Bond (New York: Oxford University Press, 1970), 121–22.

9. Samuel Johnson, *The Lives of the Most Eminent English Poets* (Oxford: Clarendon Press, 2006), 288.

10. John Keats, *Selected Letters of John Keats*, ed. Grant F. Scott (Cambridge, Mass.: Harvard University Press, 2002), 86; William Blake, *William Blake's Writings*, 2 vols., ed. G. E. Bently Jr. (Oxford: Oxford University Press, 1978), 1:80.

11. Anton Chekhov, *Letters of Anton Chekhov*, selected and edited by Avrahm Yarmolinsky (New York: Viking, 1973), 133.

12. Leslie Moore, *Beautiful Sublime: The Making of "Paradise Lost," 1701–1734* (Stanford: Stanford University Press, 1990), 2.

13. Dustin Griffin, *Regaining Paradise: Milton and the Eighteenth Century* (Cambridge: Cambridge University Press, 1986), 37.

14. Patrick Hume, *Annotations on Milton's "Paradise Lost"* (London, 1695), 2.

15. Johnson, *Lives of the Most Eminent English Poets*, 283.

16. Roy Flannagan, ed., *The Riverside Milton* (Boston: Houghton Mifflin, 1998), 303.

17. David Damrosch, ed., *The Longman Anthology of British Literature* (New York: Longman, 1999), 1731.

18. John Guillory, "Canon," in *Critical Terms for Literary Study*, ed. Frank Lentricchia and Thomas McLaughlin (Chicago: University of Chicago Press, 1990): 233–49, 237.

19. Ibid., 238.

INDEX

academic institutions, 139,
144–49, 161–62, 185–86n10.
See also education
Addison, Joseph, 1–2, 57, 60, 122,
159
admonitory exemplum, 60, 69
adventitious image, 111–15
aemulatio, 4, 11, 126
Aeneid: allusions to, 42–46, 51;
Christian epic and, 77;
episodic imitation and, 78–79,
80; originality and refinement
and, 98–102. *See also* Virgil
Aeschylus, 65, 141, 142
allusion: echo and, 31–32;
functions and effects of, 36–38,
57; historical moment and,
42–54; and Homeric source,
168–70; as indirect reference,
27–31; intertextuality and,
16–26; as learned reference,
27–31; meaning generated by,
83–89; "meaningless," 89–92;
phrasal, 81–83; spur and reprise
and, 34–35; study of, 2–7;
terminology for, 32–34; transumptive, 110–11, 114; types
of, 27–31; understanding of
term, 64–65; in war in heaven,
60–64, 70–71
Alter, Robert, 34
"ambrosial night," 47–50
"anxiety of influence," 103–04
apophrades, 108, 110, 114

Ariosto, Ludovico, 66, 107
Atkins, Samuel D., 165

Barrow, Samuel, 121, 133
Ben-Porat, Ziva, 34, 35, 52
Blake, William, 159
Blessington, Francis, 78
Bloom, Harold: criticism of,
182nn28, 29; on Johnson and
Milton, 109–16; originality
and, 10, 103–09, 117; on verbal
echoes, 6, 14
Bogan, Zachary, 42
Boileau, Nicolas: Brody on, 124;
*querelle des anciens et des
modernes* and, 133–34; on
similes, 115; on simplicity,
125; sublimity and, 11, 121
Bowen, James, 151
Brody, Jules, 123, 133

Caillois, Roger, 15
canonicity. *See* literary canon
Carew, Thomas, 107
Casaubon, Meric, 134–35
Castelvetro, Lodovico, 100
Chapman, George, 99, 133
Chekov, Anton, 159
Christian epic: criticism of,
178n3; episodic imitation and,
78–81; introduction to, 75–76;
literary survival and, 160–61;
"meaningless" allusions and,
89–92; overview of, 9–10;

189

3 5282 00718 3281